In for Dinner

In for Dinner

Rosie Kellett

101 delicious, affordable recipes to share

Clarkson Potter/Publishers
New York

For my grandmas, Pat & Margaret:
you have collectively mothered 8 children,
28 grandchildren, 10 great-grandchildren,
and counting.
You taught me how to cook, how to feed,
and how to love.
This book is for you.

To my warehouse family:
every day I thank my lucky stars I get to live
with you, cook with you, and eat with you.
Unit 16 forever.

x

In for Breakfast

In for Lunch

In for Dinner

In for Cakies

Introduction

This cookbook is a love letter to food, community, friendship, and family. It's for that big house share who each have their own bottle of olive oil but could so easily be sharing. For couples who love to host their friends and are always looking for an excuse for a dinner party. For families who want to eat delicious, affordable food but get stuck in a rut with the same recipes on repeat. For those people who live alone and want new and interesting ways to feed themselves. It's for students on a budget, hoping to make their money go that little bit further. This book is for everyone, but the people I have really written it for are those who feel intimidated by cooking for big groups, who shudder at the idea of making pasta for ten on a vacation. I want to give those cooks the confidence to make a casual chili for all their friends on a Wednesday night, because in reality, it's achievable—and cheaper!—if you know how.

"Who's in for dinner?"

Every day, I, or one of my six housemates, will ask this question on our group chat. We've been living communally for five years, cooking, eating, and planning weekly food shops together, each one of us pitching in about $30 for the week. Every night there will be a delicious meal on the table that caters to the needs and dietary requirements of whoever is in for dinner.

This book's journey to becoming a physical object is an unconventional one, shaped by the way in which we approach home life. It was created with communal living in mind and is filled with recipes inspired by all corners of the globe, representing the international makeup of our house. Our housemates collectively share a heritage that stretches from the UK to Italy, Denmark, Germany, Poland, Southeast Asia, and beyond. The book is a patchwork of staple dinners from the warehouse where my housemates and I reside, my personal family recipes, passed down through generations, and staff food concoctions that have stayed with me well past my shifts in professional kitchens, which I have been working in for the past decade.

When I think of home, I think of food. Of cold hands warmed over the stove, of stacks of hot buttered toast, of crumpets swimming in pools of salted butter, steaming bowls of porridge topped with stewed raspberries while a steady patter of snow falls outside. My fondest memories are punctuated by food—that green onion shrimp pancake my housemate Pier fed me as I collapsed at the warehouse kitchen

table, having just moved for the seventh time that year. The macaroni cheese my mum made for dinner in the dead of winter when everyone was tired, hungry, and sad.

When I think of food, I think of community. Of big family gatherings when all the aunties, uncles, and cousins would pile into someone's living room, kitchen, or hallway to eat until we could eat no more. I think of my Grandma Pat's baking, her recipes passed down through the family that are a gateway back to my youth; sticky hands, teeth glued together by her "crunch," and being offered another piece for the drive home. I'm from a big family, one of four kids, just like my parents' respective families. We are a family obsessed with food: the running joke is that while we're eating breakfast, we are thinking about lunch, and while we're eating lunch, we are discussing dinner, and if after dinner we aren't talking about what we might eat for breakfast the next day, well then, something must be wrong.

Having baked with my grandmas as far back as I can remember, in secondary school I persuaded my mum to let me cook tea for the family one night a week. I grew up calling the evening meal tea, and I always thought this was to do with where I lived, in Derbyshire; however, I have recently learned that it is to do with the British class system (more on this later). My parents are both musicians and often worked in the evenings, so we established a routine whereby once a week I would cook tea while my mum taught cello, so that we could all sit down to eat as soon as she finished. Clever parenting on my mum's part: this must have been a big help to her, while making me feel like I had won the lottery. Cooking for six soon became second nature.

It's no surprise, then, just how difficult it was to move to London in 2011, with no friends or community. It was a far cry from eating with a crowd every night, sharing our days with each other, good or bad—while finding my feet in the city, I ended up living alone for the first time in my life and missed the company of others terribly. Thankfully I quickly found work as a nanny and remember vividly how one of the mums I worked for told me that it takes seven (!) years to feel at home in London. At the time I was disheartened, but a decade on, I think she was right. It took me various living arrangements and just over six years to find my spot—through the ensuing years I was also clocking up experience in professional kitchens, from Meringue Girls, where I honed my baking skills, to working as Claire Ptak's PA at Violet Bakery, and eventually settling in the kitchen team at e5 Bakehouse, where I learned how to scale and cook delicious food for large numbers. I've lived all over

London; from four years in a guardianship flat on the edge of Hampstead Heath, north London, with a boyfriend who survived on oven fries and BLTs, to a flea-ridden house in Catford, south London, and a moldering flat share in Walthamstow, northeast London.

And then, one cold and drizzly day in March 2020, off the back of a challenging breakup, I came across a listing for a place in an East London warehouse. In Unit 16, the place I now call home, we've eaten and cooked the majority of our meals communally for the last five years. And we have eaten well, my god we have eaten well. What felt like a last resort, an "I'll take anything" viewing, from the depths of the internet, was soon to become my London home. Little did I know, I was walking into the next chapter of my life, about to meet a group of people who would become the dearest of friends and a way of life that would ultimately lead me to writing the introduction to this book today. These new friends, whom I barely knew, took me in, scooped me up, and nurtured me back to myself again. Living this way gave me a new lease on life. There is a security and a comfort to knowing there is always some-one in the house, someone to come home to and share a meal with. As with many big cities, London is undoubtedly a tough place, and it's only getting harder to build a good life here—without the warehouse I'm not sure I would still be in the city.

The Warehouse

Living communally can take many different forms. For us it means that each week we pay $30 into a kitty (a shared bank account), and that money takes care of all our household costs for the week. I'm talking food, drinks, cleaning materials, toiletries, and household goods. Then each night of the week, one person cooks dinner for everyone. We also all have a house chore each, which takes care of the recycling, fridge organization, food shopping, house laundry, and DIY. We all have different dietary requirements, but we work around each other and make sure there is always something for everyone to eat. Each day, the person cooking asks on our group chat who's in for dinner, so they know how many to cook for. If you are out but you'd like food when you get home, you can ask for a "late plate," and when you get home there will be a plate of food with your name on it, waiting for you, on the kitchen table. To stay within budget, we cook mostly vegetarian food with a little bit of fish—so the recipes in this book reflect this. We often have friends join us for dinner—this seems to fit into the budget without anyone needing to pay more.

Aside from the obvious financial benefits of living this way, knowing that my food budget for the month is $120—a difficult feat in London—this way of living has vastly improved my life. I have more time to focus, knowing that there is a delicious meal waiting for me in the evening, not having to worry about what to cook every night of the week. Everyone makes more of an effort on their night to cook, since they only do it once a week. Our sense of community and the physical act of sitting around a table, sharing a meal with one another, and the daily acts of caretaking that are woven into our life, have been transformative for my physical and mental health. Put simply, community is at the heart of our home and sharing food together each night is the linchpin of that. Your own home probably looks a little different from this, perhaps living alone or in a smaller group. To reflect our home, most of the recipes in this book are written with 6-8 people in mind—they are perfect for hosting big groups, but also ideal if you like to batch cook and prep your meals for the week without compromising on flavor, excitement, or variety. In the How to Use This Book section on page 17 I have gone into detail about how to scale a recipe up or down, so you can cook according to your needs.

Rules of thumb

Through sharing a little about our way of life on the internet and in print, I have encountered a lot of curiosity, which has prompted me to investigate how we really do make it work, because understandably people are curious—perhaps even skeptical. There are a few reasons why I think this $30 per person, per week budget works for us:

· We eat a mostly vegetarian diet with a little bit of fish.
· We shop mostly house-brand items in bulk at the most affordable supermarket.
· We do a once-weekly online shop, delivered to the warehouse, rather than lots of smaller trips throughout the week.
· There are seven of us contributing $30 to the weekly budget, and the bigger the group, the further the money goes.
· We make a lot of things from scratch! We tend not to buy packaged, premade items such as flatbreads, crumpets, granola, and pastry—we get the ingredients and make our own.
· Where appropriate, we buy frozen fruit and vegetables that can be stored and that last for longer.

Our food ethos

As a household, our calendar and the passing of time is marked with food. For example, my housemate Brandon likes to think there are two distinct seasons in a year: hot dog season (spring and summer) and lasagna season (autumn and winter). And so, as the nights draw in and the temperature drops, usually around October, we will throw a Hot Dog Lasagna Night, celebrating the end of Hot Dog Season, with a crispy onion-adorned hot dog as a starter and moving on to a perfectly crisp, layered, comforting lasagna to welcome in Lasagna Season, the recipe for which you can find on page 209. Just the same, when the days start to become longer and the weather warmer, we celebrate the changing of the seasons the other way around. This is a bizarre tradition, but one that I love and will be carrying with me to all my future homes, through the rest of my life.

The warehouse is home to our seasonal Supper Club, celebrating the very best of the season's harvest in the most delicious Italian recipes. My housemate Virginia and I host sixty-four (!) guests, over two nights, on a long communal trestle table running the length of our building, adorned with reclaimed linen napkins, tapered candles, and delicate flowers. The whole operation is a family affair, from our friends, cousins, and housemates in the kitchen, behind the camera, running the bar, to Virgi's mum flying in from her home in Reggio Emilia, Italy (the home of Parmigiano-Reggiano), for the occasion. Our warehouse is also home to a number of artists' studios, occupied by painters, set designers, and sculptors. For our suppers we collaborate with an artist on the tablecloth and exhibited art, often working with one of our resident studio holders. My sister Lily makes the prints for our posters, with our friend Frida taking care of the digital design. A carefully curated playlist of Italian bangers blasts out of our little speaker, and each time we marvel at the thrill of turning our house into a restaurant for the night.

The year is rounded off by a Christmas party, where we invite all our friends and family round for an evening of food and drinks, our trestle tables piled high with focaccia (page 110), cheese, olives, anchovies, Masala Chai Shortbread (page 231), rocky road (page 241), and panettone. Our housemate Wojciech makes a vat of mulled wine, gently warming on the stove, spiced with clove-studded oranges and fistfuls of brown sugar.

Delicious food on a budget

In this book, I promise you 101 recipes that are affordable, achievable, and good for you and for the planet alike. Recipes that will feed you and your loved ones year round, from breakfast and lunch, right through to dinner and dessert. I spent a year testing, tweaking, retesting, and feeding them to hundreds of people—filling Unit 16 with mountains of pancakes, cookies, pots of pasta, and loaf upon loaf of focaccia in search of the perfect bite for each dish. In between the covers of this book, there's a recipe for every kind of occasion: from big feasts with friends, to the perfect breakfast sandwich, small solo dinners on the sofa, slow Sunday bakes, and pizza party nights. Informed by a decade of hand-to-mouth living, my motto is that delicious food is always possible, on any budget. The key to making it work for us is that we buy in bulk, from an affordable supermarket, eat seasonally where possible, and serve a variety of meals, from super-cheap budget options to more indulgent dinner party feasts. It can't be Hot Dog Lasagna Night every day of the week, and similarly, we all need a break from baked beans every once in a while—variety is the spice of life.

While I know that living this way isn't available to everyone, I believe that sharing food at home is the best way to eat, and I hope it inspires you to find more of those moments in your own life. To help you get started, I have shared all my top tips on cooking for big groups, hosting on a budget, ingredients to invest in, and how to scale a recipe up or down. I've been cooking for large groups at home and professionally in the kitchen for over a decade, so I have a head start. For me, it has always been food. It is the thing I go to bed thinking about, and the thing I wake up thinking about. It's what I turn to when I am sad, when I'm mad, happy, drunk, or in love. I want to share my knowledge, my passion, and my recipes with as many people as possible, so that more of us can be in for dinner, more of the time.

Given the choice between dinner out or dinner in, I would always choose to stay home and cook. You will find me, always and forever, *In for Dinner*.

Cooking for big groups, a cheat sheet

Picture the scene—it's coming up to Easter, and for some reason you have been nominated to host a get-together, a brunch, a full-blown three-course meal, whatever it might be; this is how you cope.

1. Prepare as much as you can in advance

This book is full of recipes that you can make the day before serving and finish off in the moment. The more you can do before people arrive, the better, so that you can actually enjoy yourself without having to worry about the contents of that pan on the stove burning.

2. Ask for help

No person is an island; the more hands on deck the better. If there is a bunch of peeling and chopping to be done, rope in a friend, catch up while you both cry onion tears, and get the job done in half the time while you are at it. Cooking with friends is more fun, less work, and takes the pressure off what can be a difficult time already.

3. Choose the easy way out

If you are catering for a big group, there's often a nut allergy, a vegan, two gluten-free, and five carnivores; however, do not ever feel like you have to make five different meals to keep everyone happy. I often find myself catering to groups like this in the warehouse and my tactic is this: start with a base meal that everyone can eat, which will make up most of the plate, then make a few optional additions that your guests can choose from. For dessert I like to make a few bakes that when combined will keep everyone happy. It's very easy and very effective to make a little dessert table that everyone can help themselves from, and these can usually be made a few days in advance, so all you need to provide is a serving spoon and a stack of plates.

4. Don't overcomplicate things

There is no big secret to good hosting—the simple, obvious things are always the most effective. Instant added value and atmosphere can be found in good music, a lit candle, a flower in a jam jar, and a napkin, be that a folded kitchen towel or ironed linen.

Having said all the above, my biggest hope is that this book helps you enjoy cooking more than you did before, and converts a few reluctant cooks into enthusiastic hosts, which can only come from truly enjoying yourself. So have fun, make these recipes your own, and invite your friends round for dinner!

How to use this book

With the exception of baking, I am not someone who follows a recipe step by step very often. So it feels a little odd to write down a hundred and one of them, put them into a book, and ask other people to follow them. I am now an instinctual cook and generally decide what to make based on what is in the house, what is in season, how many people are in for dinner, and what their dietary requirements are. I want to encourage more people to learn to cook this way, to teach you how to look in the pantry and whip up something heavenly out of next to nothing. One important note: staying authentic to how we cook in the warehouse, I have written the recipes to feed 6–8 people, but they are all completely adaptable and I have included some advice on how to scale (see page 19). I hope these dishes will give you a nudge in the right direction, so that you are not lost without a recipe when called upon to make a quick pasta. I have offered substitutions throughout, if you don't eat or don't have certain ingredients, but I hope you will discover your own versions through trial and error. For example, wherever white wine vinegar features as a minor component in a recipe, in a pinch, red wine vinegar, apple cider vinegar, sherry vinegar, or even lemon juice will do just fine. Likewise, I have found that in most places where an anchovy is called for, white miso paste is an excellent vegan alternative.

If you'll allow the contradiction, I'd like to invite you to read the important notes below, which I think will help you enjoy cooking from this book more. But I will also encourage you to make your own decisions, have confidence in your skills, and implement changes that make sense for you.

Before you begin

Please, *I beg you*, read the whole recipe first—I promise it will save you time and hassle. Reading the recipe from start to finish is almost the equivalent of doing a lap at a party. You want to assess the scene, make sure your ex isn't lurking in the corner, so you can dive in and have fun from the get-go. If you start making the Burnt Basque Cheesecake (page 246) a few hours before you want to serve it, but haven't spotted that it needs to cool down and sit in the fridge, ideally overnight, then you are pretty much screwed. No one wants to eat hot cheesecake, and no one should have to.

Cooking times

I haven't included start-to-finish cooking times for each recipe because I frankly don't think they are ever all that accurate or useful. We all cook on a different stovetop and oven, are catering to different-sized groups, and work at a different pace. So I don't want to mislead you by claiming that a pasta will take 30 minutes to make and then for it not to work that way for you. If you are an underconfident cook and a recipe says it takes 20 minutes, but if after 15 minutes you have only just finished chopping your onions, you will feel like you have failed—and I don't want that for you. However, some of the recipes are an overnight situation, or may take several hours where you wouldn't expect them to (I'm looking at you, granola!). So I have tried to highlight the most important time considerations in the introductions and have broken down all the chapters into subchapters that indicate their time commitment, such as Speedy Salads and A Weekend Project. This, I hope, will give you all the information you need to make an educated decision.

Scaling a recipe

The recipes in this book are designed to be eaten in groups, with friends and family, but that isn't to say that you can't cook them for fewer people, or just for yourself. If a recipe says it feeds six, you could make the whole thing for two people and use the rest as meal prep for later in the week—heaven. If you don't have great fridge or freezer storage and you don't want to cook in such large quantities, then all of these recipes can be halved or even quartered. Or if you really are cooking for a crowd, they can of course be doubled and tripled too! One thing to bear in mind when scaling a recipe, up or down, is that the cooking time will vary. A note of caution: if it's a cake, for instance, with a cooking time of 40 minutes, and you want to halve the recipe, I would check after 20 minutes and again every 5 minutes until it is done.

Mise en place

My friends make fun of me whenever I say this, but I don't care. This French phrase, meaning "putting in place" or "setting up," is the linchpin of good cooking. The idea being that you gather and assemble all the ingredients, in their described prepared forms, before turning the gas on. So, if the ingredients list calls for finely diced onions and minced garlic, you need to have diced and minced before the olive oil hits the pan, otherwise your oil will have burned before you have had time to wipe the onion tears from your eyes.

Trust your gut

I have tried my best to always describe what a recipe should look, feel, smell, or sound like, as well as writing a cooking time and temperature. While the latter are important, we all use a different oven, a different stovetop, and a variety of pans, pots, and baking sheets. Your medium-high heat might be different from my medium-high heat, therefore cooking times will vary and it's important to learn a sense of what a recipe should look like as well as following the cooking times. If a cake calls for an hour in the oven, but it comes out wobbly, pale, and still wet in the middle, it probably needs a little longer. Use your gut instincts to guide you and you will learn quickly how to tell if something is ready. I know my oven: she runs hot up top and will likely burn a cake before the middle has cooked, requiring me to foil it halfway through and add up to 20 minutes on to the cooking time. Get to know your oven, and if you are really keen to be accurate, invest in an oven thermometer to get a real read on the situation.

Dietary requirements

Plant-based

Most recipes in this book can easily be made vegan—look out for the VG code in the footer of the page, which means they already are or can be made plant-based either by leaving out an ingredient or substituting an alternative. I have pointed out these substitutions along the way, but in general, dairy milk can be substituted with oat milk, dairy butter can be substituted with a plant-based butter (always try to use one that comes as a block and is labeled for baking). Where I have specified "a butter/milk of your choice," that means I have tested with both dairy and nondairy options, and they have both worked well. In most baking recipes, like in my banana loaf recipe (page 42), a flax/chia "egg" is a great substitution for a hen's egg. When I first adapt a recipe to be plant-based, I usually start by making it exactly as written in the recipe but with plant-based ingredients, and nine times out of ten this works really well. Sometimes an ingredient will behave differently from its counterpart, and that's when you have to experiment a bit more, but there is nothing more satisfying than when you get it right!

Gluten-free

Lots of the recipes in this book are naturally gluten-free; look out for the GF code in the footer of the page to easily spot which ones. It's important to note that oats are naturally gluten-free but are often handled in a factory that processes wheat, so the risk of contamination with gluten is high. If you are cooking for someone with celiac disease, make sure to use oats labeled "gluten-free." You will learn quite quickly which recipes can be substituted with gluten-free flour, although none of the sourdough or bread recipes in this book will work with an alternative, as gluten is an integral component in those recipes. However, lots of the cakes, cookies, and desserts should work well with a gluten-free flour, as they are less reliant on the production of gluten. Experiment with what works and make notes along the way.

A note on substitutions

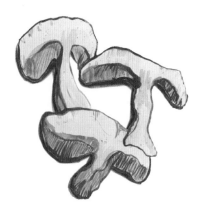

Every single recipe in this book has been written with deliciousness in mind, while balancing the need for affordability, seasonality, and accessibility. In most cases I have leaned on the more accessible and affordable ingredient, but there are a few cases where I have called for something you may be less familiar with, in the name of authenticity or when it's the most delicious ingredient for the job. In these cases I will always give an alternative: for example, in the Tofu Larb recipe on page 87 I have listed palm sugar in the ingredients. You may not find it in your corner shop, but it will be in abundant supply at any Asian grocery store, and failing that, you can always use brown sugar. Same for the buttermilk in the Blueberry Cornmeal Muffins on page 41—for me it is crucial to the flavor, but I have provided a little hack as an alternative: using the same quantity of plain yogurt mixed with 1 teaspoon of lemon juice. There is a particularly good cheese scone recipe that specifies Comté, but you will see that you can substitute with a sharp Cheddar.

My point is this: where possible I recommend using what I have written, but if you can't find, afford, or don't like the ingredient, then use your best judgment to substitute and make the recipe your own. The Brothy Fregola recipe on page 136 is one of my favorite pasta recipes in the book and is completely perfect made with fregola, but will work just fine with orzo, and if that is all you can find, then I would rather you made it with orzo than not make it at all.

Ingredients to invest in

There are a few things that I think every kitchen should have and should prioritize in terms of cost and quality. Olive oil and sea salt are top of the list; they will be in almost every recipe you make, so it's worth getting the good stuff: I'm talking about extra-virgin olive oil, and flaky sea salt rather than iodized table salt. Similarly, an investment in good-quality dairy and eggs will improve the flavor of your cooking no end. As with most of the recipes in this book, the star of the show is often vegetables, fruit, or legumes. If a recipe's main component is a bean, try to buy the best quality you can find. With canned tomatoes, the flavor difference between the cheapest option and the slightly more expensive can is really quite stark. A good can of tomatoes will add boundless flavor to your meals and is worth the investment. When it comes to fresh produce, if you try to buy what is in season and what is grown locally, not only will it be more delicious, but it will be cheaper too. The less distance your fruits and vegetables have traveled to make it onto your table, the better for both you and the planet.

For the keen baker

Sourdough starter

If you, like many, took up sourdough bread baking during the pandemic, then you may well have a starter sitting at the back of your fridge, and a basic understanding of how to care for one. A few of the recipes in this book call for sourdough starter or discard. Most sourdough bakeries will sell you a small pot of starter for you to feed and nurture at home. If not, you can make your own with patience and time over the course of a few weeks. Once you have your starter, if you are planning to bake with it regularly (and by that, I mean multiple times a week) you should keep it at room temperature and feed it once daily.

Feeding your starter

This requires you to scoop out two-thirds of the starter, put this into a sealed container, and store it in the fridge—this is your sourdough discard. To the remaining third of the starter, add an equal amount of flour and warm water. I like to do 50g of each, stir well, and cover, again leaving at room temperature. You can use a variety of flours for feeding. I tend to go with bread flour, as it's the most reliable and easy to work with, but you can experiment with wholegrain or rye flours for a more interesting color and flavor. Your starter is now fed for the day. If your starter can double in height, within 8 hours, it should be healthy enough to make bread with. If you know you won't be baking with your sourdough starter for a while, store it in the fridge until you need it, giving it a few days of feeding before you make the recipe, so that the starter is lively and active for when you would like to bake.

Levain

If you are going to make a loaf of bread, like the focaccia recipe in the In for Lunch chapter, you will need to make a levain the day before you want to bake. To do that, when you go to feed your starter, rather than discarding the scooped-out part, use it as the base of your levain (the pre-ferment for your loaf of focaccia). If a recipe calls for 100g of strong white levain, you will make this by mixing 25g of starter with 50g of bread flour and 50g of warm water. This levain is left out at room temperature overnight and then added to the dough in the morning, ultimately being used as a leavening agent in the bread.

Sourdough discard

When a recipe calls for sourdough discard, it is referring to the container in your fridge, full of the discarded starter that you have been accumulating from feeds. You can use this discard in lots of ways: head to the pikelets, pancakes, and banana loaf recipes in the In for Breakfast chapter. If a recipe just calls for sourdough discard, you can use it straight from the container in the fridge, without feeding or refreshing; using it this way will mostly be adding flavor.

The weather

An important consideration when making sourdough bread is the temperature of your kitchen and the weather outside. The rate of fermentation in sourdough is much quicker in warm weather, and much slower in the winter months. So in summer you will find your starter will double in size in far fewer hours and your dough will become bubbly and jiggly far quicker. In the winter months you will need to be more strategic about where you leave your starter and dough to ferment; a warm spot like near a radiator is ideal.

Dietary information

Dietary information can be found in the footer of each recipe using the below code, and any substitutions required are provided in the ingredients list.

GF—Gluten-Free
P—Pescatarian
V—Vegetarian
VG—Vegan

In for Breakfast

If, like me, you are a morning person, then I hope you will get a lot out of this chapter. In the warehouse we are a clean split between early risers and night owls, half of us up and at it before 8am and the others rising at the very last minute, magically out of the house in the time it takes me to make my morning coffee. There is something about the simplicity of traditional breakfast foods that I just love. In our house, granola is a big hit (a batch-cook hero, cheaper and more delicious than anything you'll get from the store), along with porridge in the wintertime and pancakes on a lazy Sunday. Beyond this, our tastes are quite eclectic and unique to each housemate. Virginia likes to have freshly squeezed orange juice every morning, and without fail will lament the quality of the citrus here compared to those from her Italian home. Pier can often be found having a miso soup or fried eggs over rice, being more of a savory guy in the morning. Wojciech and I love a pink grapefruit and Tom will regularly make himself a bagel sandwich.

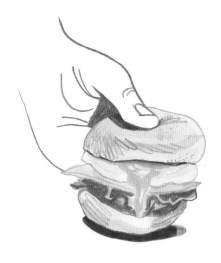

The morning is my favorite part of the day, and I love nothing more than getting tucked into bed at 10pm with my book and a sleepy tea, so that I can bounce out of bed the next day around 6am and get cracking. Similarly, breakfast is my favorite meal of the day, but ironically, I don't often get to eat it. When I start work at 7am, it feels too early to eat a meal and only a strong black coffee will do. Then I find myself getting through the first few hours of the day on adrenaline and caffeine, before I start to taste and snack on various things from the kitchen. I end up hustling through most mornings this way until I get to 1pm and realize I am ravenous and must eat immediately. I don't condone this way of behaving, it's certainly unhealthy and a habit I need to ease out of. Still, I relish my early starts: there is something so pleasing about cycling through the city as the sun rises, knowing everyone else is still sound asleep, on your way to prepare for a breakfast service. I have a theory that all cooks, chefs, and hospitality types are deep people-pleasers to their core, and that caring for and nourishing others is something that sustains us. I spend a lot of time fantasizing about what I will make for myself on the weekends, when I have more time and a slower start to the day.

To batch cook and elevate your weekday mornings
· The Granola
· Spring Summer/Autumn Winter Oats
· Korean-Inspired Marinated Eggs
· Confit Cherry Tomatoes & Labneh on Toast
· Blueberry Cornmeal Muffins

Baked goods to add to your repertoire
· Caramelized Banana Loaf
· Cheddar, Jalapeño, Chive Corn Bread with Maple Harissa Butter
· Date, Walnut & Oat Soda Bread
· Comté, Green Onion & Sesame Scones

Hearty plates to feed a crowd
· Hot Harissa Shakshuka
· Savory Corn French Toast with Cherry Tomato Salsa
· Sourdough Pancakes & Roasted Seasonal Fruit

Slow Sunday saviors to take your time over
· Semi Sourdough Pikelets
· Savory Buckwheat Galette
· Egg, Cheese, Anchovy, Spinach Breakfast Muffin
· Brown Butter Mushroom Toast with Chives, Parmesan & Lemon Dressing

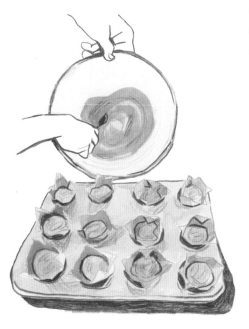

The Granola

Granola is one of those things that everyone has a strong opinion on, especially me! I want it to be crisp and caramelized, almost to the point where you question whether maybe it's too dark, but then you taste it and realize it's in fact perfect. I definitely don't want raw untoasted nuts. I DO want a hint of sweetness, but not too much. And there absolutely has to be a salt hit somewhere. This recipe delivers on all those qualities and, paired with some fruit and a splash of milk, is the perfect everyday breakfast. This batch usually lasts a week in the warehouse but is great to meal prep and can be stored for up to 6 weeks. You bake it low and slow (it really does take 100 minutes!), which is all part of the process—by investing a couple of hours of your day, you will save time, money, and effort in the long run. Shout-out to Stella Parks for the brilliant idea of soaking the oats prebake; it's a game-changer.

Makes roughly 2½ lb of granola

For the oat mix:

3½ cups rolled oats, preferably extra-thick

7 tbsp flaxseeds

2½ tbsp chia seeds

1 cup milk of your choice

½ cup (1 stick) butter of your choice, melted

¾ cup dark brown sugar

1 tsp sea salt

For the fruit and nut mix:

1 cup pumpkin seeds

7 tbsp whole almonds

7 tbsp sesame seeds

¾ cup walnut pieces

1 tsp olive oil

½ tsp sea salt

1⅔ cups dried cranberries (or your favorite dried fruit)

1. Preheat the oven to 350°F and line a baking sheet and a sheet pan with parchment paper.
2. In a large bowl, combine the rolled oats, flax, and chia seeds. Stir in the milk and melted butter until well combined. Cover and set aside to soak for 25 minutes.
3. Add the sugar and salt to the soaked oats, mix until well combined, cover, and set aside for 15 minutes.
4. Meanwhile, roast the pumpkin seeds, almonds, sesame seeds, and walnuts on a lined baking sheet in the oven for 10 minutes, until toasted and fragrant. Remove from the oven and lower the temperature to 300°F.
5. Transfer the toasted nuts and seeds to a large bowl and toss with the oil, salt, and dried fruit.
6. Put the soaked oat mix on a lined sheet pan and spread out into an even layer. Bake for 100 minutes, taking the pan out every 25 minutes to toss and turn the oats. We are baking the granola low and slow to draw out all the moisture, so make sure to set your timers; it really does need 100 minutes. When tossing and turning, you want to try to rotate the oats so that the edges go back into the middle of the pan and everything browns as evenly as possible.

(recipe continues)

7. When the oat mix is evenly golden brown and dry to the touch, transfer it to the bowl of fruit and nuts. Toss everything together, then return the mixture to a lined baking sheet to allow everything to cool completely in an even layer.

8. Once cool, store in an airtight container for up to 6 weeks.

Spring Summer/Autumn Winter Oats

Oats are one of my favorite breakfast foods and I like to eat them all year round. Below is a base recipe, with two methods for how I treat them differently depending on the season. Year round you will find a container of oats soaking in our fridge. The beauty of this is that the mix will last in your fridge for up to 5 days, so if you are feeding fewer people for breakfast, you can stretch it out over more days. I find oats are easier to digest when they have been soaked like this, and that if you are making the Autumn/Winter version, it speeds up the cooking time quite considerably. Make this vegan by using plant-based milk, and safe for celiacs by using gluten-free oats.

Serves 6

For the oats:

10 cups rolled oats, preferably
   extra-thick
1 tsp sea salt
½ tsp ground cinnamon
1 tbsp flaxseeds
1 tbsp chia seeds
4 cups water (or apple juice) to
   cover the oats and soak

To serve in spring/summer:
fresh fruit
mixed seeds
honey (or maple syrup)
nut butter
a pinch of sea salt
milk of your choice

To serve in autumn/winter:
milk of your choice
grated apple
mixed seeds
honey (or maple syrup)
nut butter
a pinch of sea salt

To make the base oat mix:
   Mix all the oat ingredients in a plastic container with a tight-fitting lid. Add enough water (or apple juice if you prefer a sweeter breakfast!) to cover the oats and stir again. Place in the fridge overnight.

In spring/summer:
   Serve a good scoop of oats topped with fresh fruit, mixed seeds, a drizzle of honey or maple syrup, a scoop of nut butter, a pinch of sea salt, and around ¼ cup of milk per portion.

In autumn/winter:
   For one portion, cook a scoop of the oat mix in a pan on the stovetop with about ½ cup of milk until the oats are tender and you have reached your desired porridge consistency. Top with grated apple, mixed seeds, a drizzle of honey or maple syrup, a scoop of nut butter, and a pinch of sea salt.

Korean-Inspired Marinated Eggs

I was introduced to marinated eggs by my housemate Pier. Occasionally he will make a big batch and keep adding freshly boiled eggs to the marinade mix over the course of the week. It was an absolute revelation to me to eat eggs this way. It feels like the ultimate umami snack: salty, sweet, fatty, and satisfying. Serve over a bowl of freshly steamed rice and you have the perfect lunch. I like to pair it with Sesame Spinach (page 160) for the ultimate happiness-in-a-bowl moment. This recipe requires a little bit of advance prep but the results will keep you stocked for days, so it's a great one to make at the start of the week and come back to when you need a speedy brunch.

Makes 12 eggs

For the eggs:
2 tsp salt
1 tbsp rice vinegar
12 eggs

For the marinade:
½ cup soy sauce (use tamari instead of soy to keep this recipe GF)
½ cup water
7 tbsp honey
3 garlic cloves, crushed
3 green onions, thinly sliced
1 green chile, thinly sliced
1 red chile, thinly sliced
1 tbsp toasted sesame seeds

For storage:
These eggs keep well in the fridge for up to 5 days, so if you make a big batch on a Sunday night you have the basis of a delicious, nutritious meal waiting for you in the fridge all week.

1. Bring a large saucepan of water to a boil and add the salt, vinegar, and eggs. Cook for 6 minutes and 30 seconds, then remove the eggs and plunge them into an ice bath. Let them cool in the ice water for at least 10 minutes—this will make them easier to peel.
2. Whisk all the marinade ingredients together in a bowl.
3. Peel the eggs and submerge them in the marinade. Store in the fridge for a few hours, or preferably overnight.
4. Serve over steamed rice, drizzled with more of the marinade, for the perfect lunch or breakfast bowl.

Confit Cherry Tomatoes & Labneh on Toast

This is my favorite way to preserve summer cherry tomatoes. It's such a treat to be able to enjoy a sugary-sweet cherry tomato, even when they are no longer in season, on top of thick, creamy labneh and perfectly toasted bread. It's a vibe any time of day, but as a slow Sunday breakfast this toast really shines. Once confited, these tomatoes will keep for up to 1 month in the fridge. Once you have made the labneh and confited the tomatoes, you can whip up this meal in seconds, so it's a great one to prep for the week and come to when you are short of time. It's not just breakfast: the tomatoes are good on everything from savory pancakes to eggs, pasta to couscous and polenta—use them far and wide! When you have eaten all the tomatoes you may well have some confit oil left over—hold on to this, as it is brilliant to add to salad dressings or use as a cooking oil, adding extra flavor to everything it touches.

Serves 4–6 as a more substantial breakfast or light brunch

14 oz (about 2⅔ cups) cherry tomatoes
¾ cup olive oil
sea salt
3 cups whole-milk yogurt
zest of 1 lemon

To serve:
6 slices of good bread (I like to use a whole wheat sourdough; use gluten-free bread to keep this recipe GF)
1 garlic clove, peeled
sea salt and black pepper

1. Put the cherry tomatoes, olive oil, and a pinch of sea salt into a medium saucepan over the lowest heat possible and leave to confit for at least 1 hour, and anywhere up to 3 hours.
2. To make the labneh, mix the yogurt with the lemon zest and ½ teaspoon of sea salt.
3. Place a sieve over a bowl and line the sieve with a large, clean piece of cheesecloth or a fresh kitchen towel. Pour the yogurt mix into the lined sieve and tuck the mixture in with the excess cloth.
4. Leave to drain like this in the fridge overnight. In the morning the bowl will have collected all the milky excess liquid from the yogurt (which you can discard), and you will have a thick labneh in the lined sieve.
5. When you are ready to serve, toast the bread and rub it lightly with the garlic clove. Top with the labneh and then the tomatoes, drizzling over some extra confit oil and sprinkling with salt and pepper.

Blueberry Cornmeal Muffins

I enjoy baking that is slightly more on the savory, rather than sweet, side. These are my answer to the classic American breakfast food: less sugary, with a lovely crunch from the cornmeal crumble topping, following in the footsteps of the Americans by utilizing buttermilk for that iconic tangy flavor. These muffins are perfect to make at the beginning of the week and keep on hand for those moments when you need something quick to grab—they freeze incredibly well, so it's always better to make the full batch, freeze half, and thank yourself later.

Makes 12 large muffins

For the muffins:
1⅓ cups / 180g all-purpose flour
1 cup / 125g fine cornmeal (or fine polenta)
⅔ cup / 125g granulated sugar
2½ tsp baking powder
1½ tsp sea salt
1⅓ cups / 200g blueberries (frozen or fresh)
2 eggs + 2 egg yolks (save the spare egg whites for the macaroons on page 225 or the pavlova on page 266)
1⅔ cups / 375g buttermilk
½ cup (1 stick) / 120g unsalted butter, melted
1 tbsp lemon zest
2 tbsp fresh lemon juice
2 tsp vanilla bean paste (or vanilla extract)

For the crumble topping:
5 tbsp / 50g all-purpose flour
3 tbsp fine cornmeal (or fine polenta)
1 tbsp powdered sugar
1 tbsp light brown sugar
a pinch of sea salt
3 tbsp unsalted butter, melted

1. Preheat the oven to 400°F, and fill a 12-cup muffin tin with extra-large cupcake liners (see the photo on the opposite page), sometimes sold as "tulip cupcake liners."
2. Whisk the flour, cornmeal, granulated sugar, baking powder, and salt in a large bowl to combine. Add 1 cup / 150g of the blueberries and gently stir until they are evenly distributed and coated in the flour mix.
3. In a separate bowl, whisk the whole eggs, yolks, buttermilk, melted butter, lemon zest and juice, and vanilla bean paste until combined. Gently fold the egg mixture into the dry ingredients until just combined, being careful not to overmix.
4. To make the crumble topping, combine all the ingredients in a bowl with a wooden spoon, until the mixture resembles large clusters.
5. Divide the batter evenly among the paper muffin liners. Top with the remaining ⅓ cup / 50g blueberries, around 3 blueberries per muffin, then add the crumble topping, gently pressing to adhere.
6. Bake for 25–30 minutes, turning the tin front to back halfway through, until a skewer inserted comes out clean.
7. Let cool in the pan before digging in.

Caramelized Banana Loaf

This humble cake got a lot of flak during the pandemic, and there was surely a moment when we all got a bit sick of it, but I have come back to its simplicity time and time again. This loaf is perfect for using up any browning bananas; when I have a whole bunch going brown, I tend to double the recipe and freeze one loaf, helping to minimize food waste and treating my future self to a banana loaf—a true gift. This version is vegan and nut-free, which is the result of tweaks made to suit the dietary needs of the warehouse. I think I actually prefer it this way, but you can easily swap the "flax egg" for two hen's eggs, and the vegan yogurt for dairy. My favorite way to serve it is lightly toasted with a little salted butter, my favorite peanut butter, and a sprinkle of sea salt.

Serves 6–8

3 ripe bananas, mashed
⅔ cup / 150g vegetable oil
1 cup / 200g dark brown sugar
2 tsp vanilla bean paste
2 tbsp ground flaxseeds (or ground chia seeds), mixed with ¼ cup water
¼ cup / 80g plain vegan yogurt
1¾ cups + 1 tbsp / 220g all-purpose flour
1 tsp baking soda
1 tsp baking powder
1 tsp sea salt
2 tbsp granulated sugar, to sprinkle on top

1. Preheat the oven to 350°F. Grease a 9 × 5-inch loaf pan and line with parchment paper.
2. Whisk together the mashed banana, vegetable oil, dark brown sugar, vanilla bean paste, flax/chia seed mixture, and yogurt, until smooth.
3. In a separate bowl, whisk together the flour, baking soda, baking powder, and salt.
4. Gently fold the dry ingredients into the wet mix and pour the batter into the loaf pan.
5. Sprinkle the top with the granulated sugar and bake for 1 hour, or until a skewer inserted comes out clean and the sugar on top is crunchy and caramelized.

Cheddar, Jalapeño, Chive Corn Bread with Maple Harissa Butter

This corn bread strikes the perfect balance of salty, sweet, and spicy—it's got a great textural crunch from the golden corn on top, and the maple harissa butter makes the whole thing sing. It's so easy to make and so very rewarding to eat. It's incredibly moist, so a loaf made at the beginning of the week will still take your breath away come Sunday (just make sure to store it in an airtight container). You could have a slice as a snack, or turn it into a meal and add sustenance with a boiled egg. Either way, it is delicious.

Serves 6–8

For the corn bread:

1 cup / 130g all-purpose flour

1⅓ cups / 180g cornmeal (or fine polenta)

5 tbsp / 70g light brown sugar

2 tsp baking powder

½ tsp baking soda

2 tsp sea salt

7 oz / 200g mature Cheddar cheese, grated

¼ cup / 70g pickled jalapeños, roughly chopped

a small bunch of chives, finely chopped

1 cup / 140g canned corn kernels

4½ tbsp / 65g unsalted butter, melted

½ cup / 115ml extra-virgin olive oil

3 eggs

1 cup / 240ml sour cream (or plain yogurt)

For the butter:

¾ cup (1 1/2 sticks) / 180g unsalted butter, softened

1 tbsp harissa

1 tbsp maple syrup (or honey)

1 tsp sea salt

1. Preheat the oven to 350°F. Grease a 9 × 5-inch loaf pan and line with parchment paper.
2. In a large bowl, whisk together the flour, cornmeal, light brown sugar, baking powder, baking soda, salt, Cheddar, jalapeños, chives, and half the corn.
3. In a separate bowl, whisk the melted butter, olive oil, eggs, and sour cream until combined.
4. Add the wet mix to the dry and fold in until just combined.
5. Pour this batter into the lined pan and sprinkle the remaining corn over the top.
6. Bake for 1 hour, or until the loaf springs back to the touch and a skewer inserted into the middle comes out dry and clean.
7. To make the butter, simply whip all the ingredients together in a bowl.
8. Serve the corn bread in thick slices, toasted and spread with the maple harissa butter.

Date, Walnut & Oat Soda Bread

Soda bread is a joy for many reasons: it requires little to no kneading, resting, or proofing, and I like to think of it as one large, abundant scone. You can whip up the dough and have it in the oven in under 30 minutes, and for that reason it's the perfect bake to accompany a midmorning cup of tea, slathered in butter and a little flaky sea salt.

Makes a large loaf

1 cup / 200g Medjool dates, pitted and roughly chopped

2 black tea bags (I like Earl Grey or English breakfast)

1 cup / 100g walnuts

4 cups / 400g white spelt flour, plus extra for dusting

½ cup / 80g semolina

½ cup / 50g rolled oats, preferably extra-thick, plus a handful for sprinkling

1 tsp baking soda

1 tsp fine sea salt

1¼ cups / 300g plain yogurt (dairy or vegan)

butter of your choice, for serving

flaky sea salt

For storage:

This soda bread is best eaten the day it is made, but it also freezes very well, so if you think you won't get round to eating the whole thing before it goes stale, just slice it up and pop it into the freezer, toasting a slice from frozen whenever you fancy it.

1. Preheat the oven to 400°F and line a baking sheet with parchment paper.
2. Soak the dates in ½ cup / 100ml of strong black tea, using both tea bags for maximum flavor.
3. Roast the walnuts on a baking sheet for 7 minutes, shaking the sheet halfway through. Once roasted, roughly chop them into similar-sized pieces to the dates.
4. Whisk the spelt flour, semolina, oats, baking soda, and fine sea salt in a large bowl until well incorporated.
5. Remove the tea bags from the date mix, reserving the liquid. Add the soaked dates to the bowl, along with all the tea, the roasted walnuts, and the yogurt. Mix well until a shaggy dough starts to form.
6. Tip the dough out onto a floured work surface. Gently and very briefly knead it until it just comes together into a consistent dough, then shape it into a ball.
7. Roll the dough ball in a handful of oats, then transfer to a lined baking sheet and score a cross on the top of the loaf, around 1½ inches deep.
8. Bake for 40–50 minutes, until golden brown and it sounds hollow when you tap the bottom.
9. Let cool on a wire rack for 30 minutes, or as long as you can bear it, then serve warm with generous amounts of butter and flaky sea salt. It's never a good idea to slice into a freshly baked loaf of bread as soon as it leaves the oven, as the inside will still be damp and gummy, so it pays to wait for at least half an hour, or ideally until it's cool to the touch.

Comté, Green Onion & Sesame Scones

In East London there is a bakery group called Pophams that does a green onion, Marmite, and cheese swirl pastry that is, put simply, life-changing. I don't have the time or the patience to make croissant dough at home, or the budget to buy one of those pastries as often as I'd like to. So I decided to take those flavors and put them into a scone. The Pophams pastry uses Schlossberger cheese—here I have used Comté, but your favorite strong hard cheese will work. My serving suggestion for these, to get the full experience, is to eat them while they are still warm, cut in half and slathered with salted butter and a healthy amount of Marmite. It's always worth making the full batch and freezing any that you don't want to bake immediately—they cook very well from frozen and it's such a treat to have them ready to bake in the freezer, for those days when you don't have time to make the full recipe from scratch.

Makes 12 scones

3 cups / 400g all-purpose flour, plus extra for dusting
1 tbsp sugar
2½ tsp baking powder
1 tsp baking soda
1 tsp sea salt
½ tsp black pepper
¾ cup (1½ sticks) / 180g unsalted butter, chilled and cubed
a small bunch of green onions, thinly sliced
¾ cup + 2 tbsp / 200g plain yogurt
1 egg, plus another beaten to use as egg wash
7 oz / 200g Comté, cubed (or your favorite sharp hard cheese, such as a mature Cheddar)
6 tbsp / 50g white sesame seeds

Equipment:

stand mixer

1. In the bowl of a stand mixer, combine the flour, sugar, baking powder, baking soda, sea salt, black pepper, and the cubed butter and mix on a slow speed with the paddle attachment. You can easily rub the butter in by hand in a large mixing bowl if you don't have a stand mixer—it will just require a little more time and energy.

2. Once the mixture resembles coarse bread crumbs, add the green onions, yogurt, and egg. Mix again until the dough has just come together.

3. Add the cubed Comté and mix for the briefest of moments until combined.

4. Turn the dough out onto a floured work surface and pat into a rough rectangle.

5. Roll the dough with a rolling pin into a long rectangle, then fold into thirds like a letter and roll out again. Repeat this step once more.

6. Line an 8 × 12-inch baking pan with plastic wrap and press the dough into the pan, until you have a flat rectangle that fills the pan. Wrap tightly in plastic wrap and chill in the freezer for 30 minutes.

7. Preheat the oven to 350°F and line a sheet pan with parchment paper.

8. Take the dough out of the freezer and turn it out onto a board. With a sharp knife, cut it into 12 equal rectangular pieces. At this stage, you can store any scones you don't want to bake in a sealed container in the freezer.
9. Brush each scone with a little egg wash and roll in the sesame seeds.
10. Place on the prepared pan and bake for 20 minutes, or until golden brown and crisp on the bottom. If baking from frozen, add 7 minutes to the cooking time.

Hot Harissa Shakshuka

I love to make this on the weekends, when I have friends round for a late breakfast. It's a real crowd-pleaser, feels quite fancy, but is in fact very easy to whip up for a big group. To make this even less labor-intensive, you can make the sauce ahead of time and store it in the fridge for up to 5 days, then reheat and add the eggs when you are ready to serve. It's also one of the more affordable recipes to make for a big group, as you are mostly relying on canned and jarred pantry staples—a winner all round!

Serves 4–6

2 onions, thinly sliced
5 garlic cloves, thinly sliced
2 tbsp olive oil
sea salt
1 large bunch of flat-leaf parsley, stems finely chopped, leaves reserved and roughly chopped
2 tbsp harissa
1 tsp smoked paprika
1 tsp chile flakes
2 tbsp tomato paste
2 (14.5 oz) cans whole peeled tomatoes
8 eggs
3½ oz feta, crumbled
black pepper
buttered toast, for serving

1. In a large shallow heavy-bottomed pan, over medium-high heat, sauté the onions and garlic in the olive oil and 2 teaspoons of salt for 10 minutes.
2. Add the parsley stems and stir to combine, cooking for another few minutes.
3. Add the harissa, smoked paprika, chile flakes, and tomato paste. Stir to combine and allow to cook for another 5 minutes.
4. Add the canned tomatoes, crushing them with the back of a spoon. Stir to combine, then simmer the sauce for 10–15 minutes.
5. Taste the sauce and adjust the seasoning if necessary.
6. Add the eggs one at a time, making a well in the sauce for each one, then cover the pan with a lid, and cook the eggs for 10–15 minutes, depending on how runny you like the yolk.
7. Sprinkle the parsley leaves and crumble the feta over the top and serve with salt, pepper, and buttered toast.

Savory Corn French Toast with Cherry Tomato Salsa

Savory will always win over sweet for me, but no more so than in a French toast recipe. This version is creamy and substantial, has an acidic hit from the salsa, and—like all the best things—is topped with a shower of grated cheese. This is one of my favorite savory breakfasts and is a great crowd-pleaser. I have to credit Stacey O'Gorman as the inspiration for this recipe—it was one of her regular lunch creations for the Meringue Girls team and I have been trying to do it justice ever since she moved back to New Zealand.

Serves 6

For the salsa:

10 oz (2 cups) cherry tomatoes, finely diced
½ red onion, finely diced
juice of 1 lime
a bunch of soft herbs: cilantro, flat-leaf parsley, dill, or a mix of all three, roughly chopped
1 green chile, finely diced, including the seeds if you like a kick
a glug of extra-virgin olive oil
a good pinch of flaky sea salt and a grind of black pepper

For the French toast:

6 eggs
1 cup canned corn kernels
1 tsp sea salt
½ tsp black pepper
½ tsp smoked paprika
6 slices of thick-cut white bread (use gluten-free bread to keep this recipe GF)
butter, for frying
2 oz strong Cheddar cheese, grated
hot sauce (optional)

1. Make the salsa first, by combining all the ingredients in a bowl and setting it to one side to marinate.
2. Crack all the eggs into a large bowl and add the drained corn, salt, pepper, and paprika. Blend the mixture with an immersion blender until silky and smooth.
3. Submerge each slice of bread in the batter to coat.
4. Heat a little butter in a frying pan over medium heat and fry each slice of bread until golden brown and crisp on both sides, adding more butter to the pan when needed.
5. Serve each slice with a little grated Cheddar, a generous helping of salsa, and perhaps some hot sauce on the side.

Sourdough Pancakes & Roasted Seasonal Fruit

I have to be honest, I'm not much of a pancake girl. You won't find me ordering a stack of American-style pancakes with maple syrup, or even a crêpe with sugar and lemon—they're just not for me. My former housemate Bee, on the other hand, adores pancakes. We would regularly find her frying a perfectly golden stack on a Sunday morning, radio on in the background, coffee in hand, quiet and content. I was determined to make a version that was savory enough for me to enjoy (the sourdough starter) and sweet enough for Bee (the roasted fruit), and that also has something interesting texturally going on (the nuts). This version uses plums, but any roasted seasonal fruit will provide a delicious, syrupy topping for your pancakes. A heads-up: the batter requires overnight prep. Turn your oven to the lowest heat and pop a plate inside to keep your pancakes warm as you fry the whole batch, so you can serve everything at the same time, piping hot.

Serves 4–6

120g sourdough starter
¾ cup milk of your choice
3½ tbsp melted butter of your choice,
    plus extra as needed
2 eggs
1 cup + 3½ tbsp all-purpose flour
1 tbsp sugar
1 tsp baking powder
1 tsp baking soda
a pinch of salt

Toppings:
yogurt of your choice
1 lb plums (or another fruit that's in
    season), pitted and halved, roasted
    with ½ cup sugar at 350°F for
    10 minutes
¾ cup almonds, lightly roasted and
    roughly chopped

1. The night before you want pancakes, make the batter. If you decide you want pancakes on the day, try to leave the batter to rest for at least 30 minutes before cooking.
2. Make the batter by whisking together the sourdough starter, milk, melted butter, and eggs until smooth.
3. In another bowl, whisk together the flour, sugar, baking powder, baking soda, and salt.
4. Whisk the dry ingredients into the wet until you have a smooth batter. Store in the fridge overnight—in the morning the batter may look a bit separated, but just give it a good whisk to bring it back together.
5. In the morning, heat a large frying pan over medium heat, melt a little butter in the pan, then fry the batter one ladle at a time, flipping after bubbles have formed on the top and the underside is golden brown, until you have an impressive stack. You may need to do this in batches, and you can keep the cooked pancakes warm in the oven, on its lowest setting, while you finish the rest.
6. Top with a generous dollop of yogurt, the roasted fruit, and a sprinkle of nuts.

Semi Sourdough Pikelets

If you aren't familiar with pikelets, let me introduce you to the fun, low-key cousin of the crumpet. To make crumpets from scratch at home, and make them well, takes a lot of time, patience, and tweaking. Pikelets, on the other hand, are quick and easy, and don't require any specialized equipment—it's just like making a pancake, except it has the texture of a crumpet—what a dream. Here I have used a little yeast to help with the texture and some sourdough discard for flavor. They freeze well and can be reheated in the toaster, just like a store-bought crumpet.

Makes 12 pikelets

100g sourdough starter (page 22)
2⅔ cups / 360g bread flour
1⅔ cups / 400g warm water
2 tsp baking powder
2 tsp baking soda
1½ tsp sea salt
1 tsp instant yeast
1 tbsp sugar
salted butter, for frying and serving
   (use a plant-based butter to keep this
   recipe vegan)

1. Whisk all the ingredients, apart from the butter, together to make a smooth batter and let rest at room temperature for 30 minutes to 1 hour.
2. Heat a large frying pan over medium heat, melt a little butter in the pan, and then add a small ladle of batter. Depending on the size of your pan, you should be able to get between 3 and 5 pikelets in at the same time. Just like with pancakes, you need to leave enough room for them to spread without touching and becoming one big pikelet, so you will need to cook the batter in batches.
3. Cook each pikelet until all the bubbles have popped on top and the surface is set and dry, around 5 minutes, then flip and allow the other side to brown, around 2 minutes.
4. Serve with plenty of salted butter and your favorite toppings—I like Marmite and cheese!

Savory Buckwheat Galette

In putting this cookbook together, what I have realized is that I LOVE a savory pancake, and this buckwheat galette features high on my list. It's the sort of crêpe you would pick up on a cobbled street in Paris for a couple of euros, the buckwheat flour giving it a deliciously nutty flavor and making it naturally gluten-free. The batter really benefits from a night of resting in the fridge, so if you can whip it up on a Saturday night, this would be the perfect slow Sunday morning meal. I like to eat one of these galettes as a light brunch, served with a salad for something more substantial.

Makes 6 galettes

For the galette mix:

1⅔ cups buckwheat flour

1 tsp sea salt

2 eggs

¾ cup milk

½ cup water

3½ tbsp melted butter, plus extra
    for frying

For the filling:

1 lb spinach

½ tsp ground nutmeg

black pepper

½ tsp sea salt

1 tsp whole-grain mustard, plus extra
    for serving

3½ oz ricotta

7 oz Gruyère (or Comté cheese),
    grated

6 eggs

a small bunch of chives,
    finely chopped

1. Whisk together the flour and salt in a large bowl. In a separate bowl, whisk together the eggs, milk, water, and melted butter.
2. Combine the wet ingredients with the dry until you have a smooth, pourable batter. Rest in the fridge, ideally overnight, or for at least 1 hour.
3. Meanwhile, to make the filling, wilt the spinach either in the microwave or by sautéing it in a frying pan over medium heat. Once wilted, squeeze out as much moisture as possible, then mix with the nutmeg, ½ teaspoon of black pepper, the salt, mustard, and ricotta.
4. When you are ready to cook and serve, turn the oven to its lowest setting (we will use this to keep the galettes warm while you cook them one by one).
5. Place a frying pan over medium heat. Melt a small knob of butter, then add a ladle of galette batter, enough to coat the pan in a thin layer. With a frosting or offset spatula, spread the batter to the edges to make a thin circular galette. Let set and cook for 2–3 minutes.
6. Loosen the edges of the galette with a spatula, sprinkle a handful of cheese into the middle of the galette, then add a scoop of the spinach mixture.
7. Fold each side of the pancake halfway into the middle, making a square galette with a window into the spinach and cheese mix in the middle (see pages 60–61).
8. Cook for another 2–3 minutes, or until the cheese is melted and oozing out of the sides.

9. Transfer the cooked galette to a lined sheet pan and keep warm in the oven.
10. Repeat with the rest of the mixture, transferring each pancake to the oven to keep warm while you cook the rest.
11. When you are ready to serve, fry an egg for each pancake.
12. Serve each pancake topped with a fried egg, sprinkled with chopped chives, more black pepper, and with whole-grain mustard on the side.

Egg, Cheese, Anchovy, Spinach Breakfast Muffin

I always think it's a cop-out to include what is essentially a sandwich recipe in a cookbook, so hear me out. This is less a recipe, more a list of suggestions, to lead you on your way to the best breakfast sandwich of your life. I am a sucker for a well-executed savory breakfast muffin, and this one was inspired by a combination of a few of my favorite weekend East London bakery treats. The below is a guide to making one muffin—it's for those slow weekends where you lie in, wake up between mealtimes, and want something easy, satisfying, but wholly luxurious. Treat yourself to this sandwich and thank me later. Having said that, this recipe is easily scaled to feed as many people as you desire; simply multiply by the number of muffins you would like to make.

Makes 1 muffin

For the salsa:
¼ shallot, finely diced
a splash of red wine vinegar
a few sprigs of flat-leaf parsley, chopped
a splash of olive oil
sea salt and black pepper

For the muffin:
1 English muffin
1 large handful of spinach
olive oil, for frying
1 egg
2 good-quality anchovies, in oil
a few slices of Comté (or sharp Cheddar)
butter of your choice, for serving
1 tsp Dijon mustard

1. Start by making the salsa: combine the shallot, vinegar, parsley, olive oil, and a pinch each of salt and pepper.
2. Toast the English muffin to perfection.
3. Wilt the spinach by sautéing it in a hot pan for a few minutes in a little olive oil. Remove and squeeze out as much moisture as possible.
4. Fry the egg in a little olive oil, and as soon as it has set enough, lay the anchovies and sliced Comté on top and cover the pan with a lid—this will melt the cheese on top of the egg as it continues to cook.
5. To assemble: lightly butter the muffin, then spread a thin layer of Dijon mustard over both halves. Add the wilted spinach, then the egg/anchovy/cheese stack, the salsa, and finally the muffin lid.
6. Devour.

Brown Butter Mushroom Toast
with Chives, Parmesan & Lemon Dressing

This is one of those recipes that uses a lot of butter—it just does, and you have to accept that at the beginning, then move on. It's the sort of breakfast that should be saved for a slow Sunday, when you are feeding a crowd and you are in no hurry to get food on the table. It's a labor of love that pays dividends in the end. The dressing cuts through all that butter perfectly, and if you have any left over it is the perfect addition to most savory foods, namely eggs!

Serves 6

For the mushrooms:
1½ lb mixed mushrooms of your
    choice (I like cremini and portobello)
¾ cup + 2 tbsp unsalted butter, cut into
    6 equal pieces
2 tsp black pepper
2 tsp flaky sea salt

For the dressing:
7 tbsp chives, finely chopped
juice of 1–2 lemons
2 tbsp olive oil
sea salt and black pepper

To serve:
a loaf of good bread (use gluten-free
    bread to keep this recipe GF)
more butter (optional)
a small piece of Parmesan, grated
    (omit to keep this recipe V)

1. Halve or quarter the mushrooms, depending on their size. You want a nice flat side to each mushroom because this is the part that will caramelize and crisp up, giving flavor and texture.

2. Melt a sixth of the butter in a large frying pan over medium-high heat. Once it is completely melted and bubbling, add roughly one-sixth of the mushrooms, cut side down in the pan. You want to cook the mushrooms in batches, and this worked out at roughly sixths for the size of pan I used. However you do it, just make sure you are using the relevant amount of butter.

3. Leave the mushrooms undisturbed in the pan for at least 3 minutes, until the underside is golden brown and crisp, then flip and cook through on the other side. Season with black pepper as you go, but do not be tempted to add any salt to the pan, as this will release all the water in the mushrooms and they will go limp and soggy, and every-one will be sad. Instead, sprinkle the mushrooms with flaky salt once cooked and out of the pan.

4. Repeat the process until you have cooked all the mush-rooms.

5. Meanwhile, make the dressing by combining all the ingredients together in a bowl.

6. When you are ready to serve, toast the bread, spread with butter if desired, pile high with mushrooms, and finish with a drizzle of the dressing and a grating of Parmesan.

In for Lunch

In for Lunch

My first encounter with communal cooking came from my job at Meringue Girls—it was my first London job and I ended up working there on and off for eight years. Part of the reason I stayed for so long was the lunches. We had a system whereby everyone brought in $2.50 a day for lunch, and each day someone would cook lunch for everyone using the budget. The bakery was just behind Broadway Market, an ever-popular and busy market street in East London, with more organic shops than it can possibly sustain. We would struggle to keep our daily team lunches going on a budget of $12 per day with the way Broadway Market is set up these days. But back in 2016 it was possible to go out and get the ingredients for a healthy, delicious, and nutritious lunch to feed five, for that amount of money. I loved this way of eating, breaking up the day to sit down together and catch up over great food, not common in many professional kitchens. I often volunteered to do the cooking and would relish starting the conversation around what to eat as early as possible—we drew the line at post 10:30am. I found it so exciting to come up with a meal based on how everyone was feeling; whether they fancied something fresh, light, hearty, or warming, I would come up with a lunch that used what we already had in the fridge and what I could get in the market.

This way of cooking, making the most of what is available, in season, and affordable, has carried through to the way we cook in the warehouse. Lunchtime is always a somewhat frantic moment in our home, and changes every day, as we all lead busy lives with varying schedules. On some weekdays you will find Pier at the stove, having made fried rice and a curry big enough to feed twenty grown adults. On these days, at the ring of the dinner bell, people magically appear from all corners of the warehouse: studio holders, house-mates, friends, whoever is close enough to get a hint of the aroma coming out of the kitchen, will find their way to the table. I strongly identify as a feeder, but I have yet to meet another soul who fits the description quite as well as Pier does. He was born to feed, nourish, and comfort people with his food. He is the most considerate of cooks, often making three versions of his cashew chicken curry—one with chicken, one with tofu, and another without the nuts—so that everyone is catered to. So, on these days, we are lucky, there will be enough hotpot, curry, sesame noodles, or eggplant rice for the whole warehouse to have a hearty lunch and there will be leftovers for whoever missed out. On other days, everyone eats at different times and does their own thing, often eating whatever can be found in the leftovers' fridge.

I've broken the recipes down into categories to help you identify at a glance the perfect lunch for you.

Speedy salads to brighten up your day through spring and summer

- Summer Holiday Bean Salad
- The Ultimate Chopped Egg Salad
- Tuna Salad
- Panzanella
- Beet, Black Lentil, Feta & Walnut Salad
- Crispy Chickpea Caesar Salad, Fennel Seed Croutons & Tahini Dressing
- Herby Vinegar-Laced Potato Salad
- Vermicelli Salad, Crispy Tofu & Satay Dressing
- Tofu Larb, Lettuce Cups, Abundant Herbs & Roasted Peanuts

Soups to batch cook and carry you through the week

- Spring/Summer Tomato Soup
- Autumn/Winter Tomato Soup
- Pearl Barley & Spring Vegetable Soup with Salsa Verde
- Roasted Carrot, Cumin & Coconut Soup with Cilantro Salsa
- Salt & Vinegar Potato Soup

Breads and pastry, to mop everything up with

- Bee's Potato Flatbreads
- Pier's Shrimp & Green Onion Pancakes
- Erbazzone Reggiano
- Potato, Mozzarella & Rosemary Galette
- Sourdough Focaccia, Three Ways

Summer Holiday Bean Salad

I have vivid memories of vacationing in Tuscany as a child and our family friend, Louisa, making this salad for lunch, with rosemary from the garden, served in the dizzying midday sun. In the summer there is nothing quite like it, but it works well as a simple lunch all year round—in winter, I like to slightly warm it up and serve it with a chunk of toasted bread. You can include a few cans of good-quality tuna for added protein, but below is the classic version. Use the best-quality canned beans you can find; they are the star of the show here and are worth the extra expense. This truly is the quickest, easiest, and most affordable of lunches—while not compromising on a drop of flavor.

Serves 6 as a light lunch

4 (15 oz) cans of your favorite beans, drained
3 sprigs of rosemary, leaves picked and finely chopped
2 garlic cloves, crushed
7 tbsp good-quality extra-virgin olive oil
juice of 2 limes
1 tbsp red wine vinegar
2 tsp flaky sea salt
1 tsp black pepper

1. Mix all the ingredients in a large bowl and allow to marinate at room temperature for at least an hour, the longer the better.
2. Serve as a main with a piece of fresh bread, or as a side. Ideally, eat in the sunshine.

The Ultimate Chopped Egg Salad

Don't be fooled, this is not your typical egg salad. For one thing, it is very light on the mayo, and for another I like to fill mine with pickled, leafy, and fresh additions that make for the most delicious sandwich filling. This one's a winner: I used to regularly make this sandwich at e5 Bakehouse, and they would always sell out before 1pm. If you're looking to mix things up, try this atop toasted rye—though it tastes pretty heavenly between cheap squashy sliced white bread too.

Makes 4 sandwiches

8 eggs
1 tbsp capers, roughly chopped
4 large dill pickles, finely diced
2 tsp Dijon mustard
2 tbsp extra-virgin olive oil, plus extra
    as needed
1 tbsp mayonnaise
a small bunch of flat-leaf parsley,
    roughly chopped
a small bunch of chives, roughly
    chopped
sea salt and black pepper

To serve:
your favorite bread (use gluten-free
    bread to keep this recipe GF)
a handful of watercress, tossed in fresh
    lemon juice and olive oil

1. Hard-boil the eggs for 10 minutes in boiling water. Drain, cool under cold water, and peel.
2. Grate the eggs on a box grater into a wide bowl.
3. Add the capers, pickles, mustard, olive oil, mayonnaise, herbs, 1 teaspoon of salt, and ½ teaspoon of pepper and give it a good mix.
4. Taste for seasoning and adjust to your taste, adding more salt, pepper, olive oil, etc., until you are happy.
5. Slice, toast, or tear your bread, make a sandwich or don't, and enjoy with lemony watercress!

Tuna Salad

A super-quick and easy lunch, less a salad and more of a sandwich filling, this is my take on the American classic. My favorite way to eat this is atop a lightly toasted everything bagel from my friends at Papo's Bagels in East London. They make the best New York–style bagels in London, serving an exceptional tuna salad sandwich in their bakery, and my versions are all made in an effort to live up to theirs. This recipe leans on good-quality olive oil for most of the fat and has a fair amount of acidity from the capers and lemon to cut through. It's excellent on its own, piled onto a toasted piece of rye bread, or served with a boiled egg for a more filling lunch. This may feel a little more extravagant than your classic tuna salad, but I promise you it's worth it.

Makes 4 sandwiches

2 (5.6 oz) cans water-packed tuna, drained
2 tbsp capers, finely diced
a large bunch of flat-leaf parsley, roughly chopped
2 oz cornichons (or pickles), finely diced
zest and juice of 1 lemon, plus extra as needed
2 tbsp olive oil, plus extra as needed
½ red onion, finely diced
2 tbsp mayonnaise
1 tsp Dijon mustard
sea salt and black pepper
bagel and jammy boiled egg, for serving

1. Combine the tuna, capers, parsley, cornichons, lemon zest and juice, olive oil, onion, mayonnaise, mustard, 1 teaspoon of salt, and ½ teaspoon of black pepper in a large bowl, mixing until well combined. Taste for seasoning and add more salt, pepper, lemon, or oil to suit your taste.
2. Slather onto a lightly toasted bagel and pair with a jammy boiled egg for the perfect lunch.

Panzanella

In summer, when tomatoes come into season, the first thing I do is slice one open, sprinkle it with a little salt, eat it whole, and die a death of happiness. The second thing I do is make panzanella. It's the perfect summer salad, letting tomatoes really shine, and it uses up your stale end-of-loaf bits of bread. Never throw those bits away; chuck them in a bag in your freezer for the moment when you get your first ripe summer tomatoes and you make this salad.

Serves 6 as a main or 8 as a side

2½ lb of the best ripe tomatoes you can find—a mix of varieties is lovely

1 tbsp sea salt

½ loaf of bread (I like to use sourdough; use gluten-free bread to keep this recipe GF), torn into bite-size pieces

½ cup extra-virgin olive oil, plus extra for drizzling

2 banana shallots, thinly sliced

2 garlic cloves, minced

3 tbsp red wine vinegar

½ tsp black pepper

a large bunch of basil, leaves picked, half thinly sliced, half reserved whole

2 tbsp capers

5 oz (about 1 cup) Kalamata olives, pitted

1. Preheat the oven to 350°F.

2. Roughly chop the tomatoes into bite-size pieces. Toss them with the salt, then transfer them to a large colander, set over a bowl, to drain for 30 minutes. The tomatoes will release a lot of their juices and the salty, tomatoey liquid that gathers in the bowl will be the base of the dressing, so don't discard this, it is liquid gold! You can weigh the tomatoes down with another clean bowl to speed along the liquid gathering.

3. While the tomatoes are draining, toss the bread with a drizzle of olive oil on a large baking sheet and toast in the oven for 15 minutes. You want the pieces to be starting to crisp up on the outside and take on a little color, but still be squashy in the middle.

4. To make the dressing, take 2 tablespoons of the salty tomato liquid in the bowl and whisk in the shallots, garlic, red wine vinegar, black pepper, and olive oil. Taste the dressing and adjust the levels of acid, fat, and salt to your liking.

5. Once you are happy, mix the tomatoes, toasted bread, sliced basil, capers, olives, and the dressing in a large bowl, until well combined. You want the bread to soak up a lot of the dressing, so let it sit for at least 5 minutes before mixing again, then serve, topped with the reserved basil leaves and a drizzle of olive oil.

Beet, Black Lentil, Feta & Walnut Salad

This salad is a lovely one to make at the start of spring, celebrating the new season's beets coming in with something fresh for lunch. Goat cheese works really well instead of the feta, and I've done this with both Puy and beluga lentils. It's one of those salads that is almost better the next day, once the dressing has really had a chance to sink in, so fear not if you have leftovers, they are tomorrow's lunch.

Serves 4 as a main or 6 as a side

1½ cups walnuts
¼ cup olive oil, plus extra for drizzling
sea salt
2¼ lb cooked beets, roughly chopped
2 cups cooked black lentils
1 banana shallot, thinly sliced
5 oz feta, cubed
a bunch of flat-leaf parsley, roughly chopped
zest and juice of 2 lemons
1 tbsp white wine vinegar
black pepper
flatbreads (or sourdough), for serving

1. Preheat the oven to 400°F.
2. Roast the walnuts in the oven until fragrant and starting to color, between 8 and 10 minutes. Drizzle with a little olive oil and sprinkle with a pinch of sea salt, then toss to combine. Set the walnuts to one side to cool.
3. In a large bowl, combine the beets, lentils, shallot, three-quarters of the feta, the parsley, lemon zest and juice, vinegar, and a good drizzle of the remaining olive oil. Toss until well combined.
4. Pile the mixture onto a large platter, scatter with the walnuts, crumble the rest of the feta over the top, and give it one last drizzle of olive oil and a good grind of black pepper.
5. Serve with warm flatbreads or toasted sourdough.

Crispy Chickpea Caesar Salad, Fennel Seed Croutons & Tahini Dressing

I LOVE Caesar salad, maybe more than any other salad! It's a big claim, but for me it has everything: crunchy texture, creamy dressing, Parmesan aplenty, and, like all my favorite lunches, it pairs perfectly with a jammy egg. This version showcases roasted crispy golden chickpeas, which add a welcome boost of protein, but feel free to substitute with your favorite protein.

Serves 6 as a side or 3 as a main

For the chickpeas:
3 (15 oz) cans chickpeas, drained and
   patted dry
2 tbsp olive oil
½ tsp sea salt
½ tsp black pepper
1 tsp smoked paprika

For the croutons:
10 slices of stale bread, torn into
   bite-size chunks (use gluten-free
   bread to keep this recipe GF)
2 tsp fennel seeds
2 tbsp olive oil
sea salt and black pepper

For the dressing:
½ cup tahini
1 garlic clove, minced
juice of 1 lemon
sea salt and black pepper

For the salad:
2 baby gem lettuces, roughly chopped
1 head of firm lettuce, roughly chopped
a small bunch of flat-leaf parsley,
   roughly chopped
2 oz Parmesan (or a hard cheese of
   your choice), finely grated

1. Preheat the oven to 350°F.
2. On a sheet pan, toss the chickpeas with the oil, salt, pepper, and paprika.
3. On a separate pan, toss the bread with the fennel seeds, olive oil, 1 teaspoon of salt, and ½ teaspoon of pepper.
4. Roast both the croutons and chickpeas in the oven for 30 minutes, tossing halfway through, until crisp and golden brown.
5. To make the dressing, whisk together all the ingredients and then thin down with ice water until you reach a creamy consistency.
6. To serve, toss the lettuces and parsley with half the dressing, then on a large platter layer the dressed salad with the croutons, chickpeas, and Parmesan. Drizzle over the remaining dressing.

Herby Vinegar-Laced Potato Salad

The great thing about growing older is realizing that a potato salad (hell, any salad) can be anything you want it to be. I've always been more inclined to the salty-sour side of things, so I started experimenting with herbs, vinegar, and other pickled additions to make the potato salad of my dreams. This version is perfectly salty, sour, and fatty, the most welcome addition at any picnic, and just gets better with time. It keeps incredibly well in the fridge, so make a batch on Monday and you will be thanking yourself throughout the week. Share it with your friends, your family, your co-workers, and spread the potato salad love far and wide.

Serves 6–8 as a side

2¼ lb new potatoes (the baby spring kind), thoroughly washed, skins intact
1 banana shallot, thinly sliced
2 green onions, thinly sliced
1 medium bunch of flat-leaf parsley, stems thinly sliced and leaves roughly chopped
1 medium bunch of dill, stems thinly sliced and leaves roughly chopped
2 pickled gherkins, finely diced
1 tbsp capers, roughly chopped
2 tsp whole-grain mustard
2 tbsp white wine vinegar
½ tsp black pepper
zest and juice of 1 lemon
¼ cup extra-virgin olive oil
1 tsp sea salt

1. Boil the new potatoes (whole) in well-salted water until cooked through and tender. This took 20 minutes for me but will depend on the size of your potatoes. They are done when a knife slides easily through the middle.
2. While the potatoes are cooking, make the dressing by combining in a large bowl the shallot, green onions, parsley and dill stems (save the leaves for later), diced gherkins, capers, mustard, vinegar, black pepper, lemon zest, lemon juice, and olive oil. Whisk to combine.
3. Taste the dressing—there are lots of salty, briny, pickled elements here so you may not need a full teaspoon of salt, so add to taste and whisk again.
4. Once the potatoes are cooked, drain and return them to the pan. I like to halve the larger ones, using a knife in the pan, then put the lid on and give them a shake to rough up the edges.
5. Add the potatoes to the dressing and mix well—adding them while they are still hot helps them soak up more of the dressing and results in a more flavorful potato.
6. Once they have cooled to around room temperature, add the parsley and dill leaves, toss again, taste, and adjust the seasoning if necessary.
7. Serve! This salad is also incredible the next day, once the potatoes have soaked up even more of the flavor from the juicy dressing.

Vermicelli Salad, Crispy Tofu & Satay Dressing

There are winter noodles and summer noodles, and this recipe is firmly the latter. On a hot summer's day this is one of my favorite things to eat for lunch, and it used to be a Meringue Girls bakery lunch staple. It's quick, healthy, and incredibly easy.

Serves 6

For the noodles:
14 oz vermicelli rice noodles
2 tsp sesame oil

For the tofu:
1 (14 oz) package extra-firm tofu
2 tbsp soy sauce*
1 tsp honey (or maple syrup)
2 garlic cloves, minced
1 tsp rice vinegar
1 tsp sriracha
1 tsp sesame oil
1 tbsp toasted sesame seeds
1 tbsp vegetable oil

For the satay sauce:
½ cup of your favorite peanut butter
2 garlic cloves, minced
juice of 2 limes
2 tsp sriracha
2 tsp soy sauce*
1 tsp honey (or maple syrup)
3 tbsp oat milk (or coconut milk if you
    have a can open)

For the salad:
1 medium cucumber, thinly sliced
1 medium carrot, thinly sliced
1 medium shallot, thinly sliced
a handful of picked mint leaves,
    shredded

* substitute with tamari to keep this
    recipe GF

1. Cook the noodles by soaking them in freshly boiled water for 4–5 minutes until tender. Drain the noodles and run under cold water until cooled, then drain again.
2. Toss the cooled noodles in the sesame oil and set to one side until you are ready to serve.
3. Press the tofu between two wads of paper towels, squeezing out as much moisture as you can, balancing a heavy pan on top to help it along.
4. While the tofu is pressing, whisk together the soy, honey, garlic, vinegar, sriracha, sesame oil, and toasted sesame seeds to make a sauce.
5. Heat the vegetable oil in a large frying pan over medium-high heat. Dice the tofu and cook in the vegetable oil until crispy and starting to color.
6. Turn the heat down to medium, then pour the sauce into the pan and toss with the tofu. Keep cooking until the sauce has thickened and reduced, around 10 minutes.
7. Meanwhile, make the satay. Whisk together the peanut butter, garlic, lime juice, sriracha, soy, and honey into a paste. Then add the oat milk and whisk until smooth.
8. Divide everything among 6 bowls, starting with the noodles, topping with the tofu, satay sauce, fresh vegetables, and mint.

Tofu Larb, Lettuce Cups, Abundant Herbs & Roasted Peanuts

Larb is a Thai dish, traditionally made with minced pork. I was introduced to it by Stacey O'Gorman while we were traveling together in New Zealand. She made a delicious version with mushrooms, and I have been obsessed ever since. While mushrooms work well, I prefer the texture of tofu and crumbling is far quicker than chopping. This salad is healthy, simple, and fresh, a real summer favorite.

Serves 6 as a light lunch

2 tbsp sticky rice (or white rice), uncooked

2 tbsp vegetable oil

2 (14 oz) packages firm tofu, pressed to release as much moisture as possible

1 tsp sea salt

1 tbsp chile flakes

1 tsp palm sugar (or dark brown sugar), plus extra as needed

1 tbsp fish sauce (omit to keep this recipe vegan), plus extra as needed

juice of 3 limes, plus extra as needed

3 banana shallots, thinly sliced

3 garlic cloves, minced

1 tbsp soy sauce (substitute with tamari to keep this recipe GF)

a small bunch of green onions, finely chopped

a small bunch of cilantro, leaves picked, and stems finely chopped

a small bunch of mint, leaves picked

To serve:
steamed sticky rice (or white rice)
lettuce cups
roasted salted peanuts

1. Toast the uncooked rice grains in a dry frying pan over medium-high heat, keeping the rice moving so it browns evenly to a deep golden brown—this will take 10–15 minutes.

2. Take the pan off the heat and grind the rice to a fine powder with a mortar and pestle or a high-speed blender.

3. To make the larb, heat the vegetable oil in a large wok. Crumble the tofu into the texture of ground meat, then add to the pan with the salt and fry for 15 minutes, until starting to color and crisp up.

4. Take the wok off the heat and stir in the remaining larb ingredients: chile flakes, palm sugar, fish sauce, lime juice, shallots, garlic, soy sauce, green onions, ¾ of each of the herbs, and the rice powder. Mix thoroughly so the tofu is evenly coated.

5. Taste the larb and adjust the seasoning, adding more sugar, lime, or fish sauce to suit your taste.

6. Serve with steamed rice, lettuce cups, more herbs and sprinkled with the salted peanuts.

Spring/Summer Tomato Soup

I had never understood cold soup until I was working in a professional kitchen and my Spanish colleague José made me a bowl of gazpacho, and later our head chef, Beta, made salmorejo. This recipe is an amalgamation of the two. I'm not such a fan of peppers, so I have left them out. I hesitate to call this gazpacho or salmorejo because it is neither, and I don't want to annoy any of my Spanish friends. So instead, I call it Spring/Summer Tomato Soup—and I hope they approve! This soup is the ideal recipe to batch make in the heat of summer and keep in the fridge, ready and chilled for when you need a light, fresh, thirst-quenching lunch.

Serves 6

about 3 lb ripe juicy tomatoes, the best you can find
1 medium cucumber, peeled, seeded, and roughly chopped
2 garlic cloves, grated
5 slices of bread, crusts removed, cut into cubes
2 tsp sherry vinegar (or red wine vinegar)
2 tsp sea salt
5 tbsp extra-virgin olive oil, plus extra for drizzling
3 eggs
a small bunch of chives, chopped
black pepper

1. Score a cross into the skin at the base of each tomato, then submerge in freshly boiled water for 10 minutes. After this, the skins should be easy to remove.
2. Once the tomatoes are skinned, take out the cores and roughly chop.
3. In a large bowl, combine the tomatoes, cucumber, garlic, bread, vinegar, salt, and half the olive oil. Scrunch everything together with your hands so it is very well mixed, then set to one side to marinate for 30 minutes.
4. Meanwhile, hard-boil and peel the eggs, then grate them coarsely on a box grater.
5. Blend the tomato mix with an immersion blender or in a blender until smooth, and continue blending while you add the remaining olive oil, until silky smooth.
6. Taste and adjust the salt and vinegar levels to your taste, then chill in the fridge until completely cold.
7. Serve in shallow bowls, topped with grated egg, chopped chives, a drizzle of olive oil, and ground black pepper.

Autumn/Winter Tomato Soup

When tomatoes are no longer in season, the days are getting shorter and the weather colder, this is my favorite speedy soup to warm up with. It's ready in under an hour and always hits the spot. There is a kick from the chile, perfectly balanced out by the yogurt, and the beans are the secret ingredient for added creaminess and sustenance. Like most soups, this freezes incredibly well, so you can always make the full batch and freeze half for another day. A wallet-, planet-, and health-friendly lunch if ever there was one!

Serves 6

4 white onions, halved
1 medium bulb of garlic, top sliced
    off to reveal the cloves
sea salt and black pepper
½ tsp chile flakes, plus extra as needed
2 tbsp olive oil
2 tbsp tomato paste
2 (14.5 oz) cans whole peeled tomatoes
1 (15 oz) can white beans, such as
    cannellini or butter beans, liquid
    included
1 vegetable bouillon cube
juice of ½ lemon, plus extra as needed
plain yogurt of your choice, for serving
chili oil, for drizzling (optional)

1. Preheat the oven to 350°F.
2. Toss the onions, garlic bulb, 1 teaspoon of salt, ½ teaspoon of pepper, the chile flakes, and olive oil in a large roasting pan. Turn the onions and garlic cut side down in the pan and roast for 40 minutes.
3. Tip the roasted alliums into a soup pot, squeezing all the garlic flesh out of their skins—be careful, they will be hot!
4. Set the pan over medium heat and add the tomato paste, canned tomatoes, and white beans with their liquid.
5. Swill a little water round the tomato cans, then add the tomato water to the pan along with the bouillon cube.
6. Bring to a boil, then lower the heat and simmer for 20 minutes, stirring occasionally to make sure the bottom doesn't catch.
7. Blend the soup with an immersion blender or in a blender until smooth, then add the lemon juice and taste for seasoning. Add more chile flakes, salt, pepper, or lemon juice, to suit your taste.
8. Serve the soup in big bowls, topped with plain yogurt, and a drizzle of chili oil if you like an extra kick.

Pearl Barley & Spring Vegetable Soup with Salsa Verde

This soup is ideal at the beginning of spring, when we still need a warming lunch but the spring produce, such as garden peas, is starting to come in. You can make it in the winter with frozen peas and it's just as good. You may have leftover salsa, and I encourage you to use it in abundance on everything from eggs, to pizza, to beans, or simply to dip fresh bread into.

Serves 6–8

For the soup:
3 tbsp olive oil, plus extra for drizzling
3 white onions, finely diced
3 carrots, peeled and finely diced
1 bulb of garlic, top sliced off to reveal the cloves
1 lemon, halved, seeds removed
1 tsp sea salt
½ tsp black pepper
1 tbsp tomato paste
¾ cup white wine
a few sprigs of rosemary and thyme
1¼ cups pearl barley
1 vegetable bouillon cube
1 tsp white wine vinegar
7 oz (1½ cups) peas

For the salsa verde:
a small bunch each of cilantro, flat-leaf parsley, chives, and dill
2 tbsp capers, plus 1½ tbsp of their brine
juice of ½ lemon
7 tbsp extra-virgin olive oil
½ tsp sea salt
½ tsp black pepper

crusty bread, for serving

1. Put the olive oil, onions, carrots, garlic, halved lemon, salt, and pepper into a large heavy-bottomed pan and place over medium-high heat. Stir to combine, then sauté for at least 20 minutes, until jammy, reduced, and beginning to color.
2. Add the tomato paste and keep cooking for 5 minutes until the color has deepened.
3. Add the white wine, rosemary, thyme, pearl barley, bouillon cube, and 4 cups of freshly boiled water.
4. Bring to a boil, then lower to a simmer for 45 minutes, stirring occasionally and topping up with more water if it looks dry.
5. Once the pearl barley is plump and cooked, add the vinegar and peas and stir to combine.
6. Fish out the bulb of garlic with a slotted spoon. Using tongs, squeeze out all the jammy cooked cloves and put them back into the soup, discarding the empty skins.
7. To make the salsa, blend everything in a high-speed blender until smooth.
8. Serve the soup in wide shallow bowls, topped with the salsa, a drizzle of olive oil, and a chunk of warm crusty bread.

Roasted Carrot, Cumin & Coconut Soup with Cilantro Salsa

Carrot and cilantro was never a soup I was drawn toward until a particular day at work in the kitchen, when I was responsible for staff lunch. There was very little to work with in the walk-in fridge, except a crate full of carrots and a sack of wilting cilantro. I was in a rush and snowed under with prep for the weekend brunch menu, so I decided to speed things up by roasting all the ingredients together. The result was far better than I could have hoped for, and now I make all my soups this way, adding a depth of flavor that is hard to achieve in a pot on the stovetop. This soup is perfectly warming, creamy, gently spiced, and ever so slightly sweet with the salsa cutting through—the perfect mouthful in my opinion!

Serves 6–8

2¼ lb carrots
3 white onions, halved
1 whole bulb of garlic, top sliced off
    to reveal the cloves
1 thumb-size piece of ginger, chopped
1 red chile, stem removed
3 tbsp olive oil
2 tbsp ground cumin
sea salt and black pepper
1 (13.5 oz) can full-fat coconut milk
2 cups vegetable stock
chili oil, for serving (optional)

For the salsa:
½ white onion, finely diced
juice of 2 limes
a small bunch of cilantro, finely
    chopped
1 red chile, finely chopped
½ tsp sea salt
1 tbsp extra-virgin olive oil

crusty bread of your choice, for serving

1. Preheat the oven to 350°F.
2. Put the whole carrots, halved onions, garlic, ginger, and red chile into a large roasting pan.
3. Toss with the oil, cumin, and a little salt and pepper. Make sure the onions and garlic are cut side down.
4. Roast in the oven for 40 minutes, or until a sharp knife cuts easily through the largest vegetable.
5. Tip the contents into a large stockpot, taking the whole bulb of garlic and squeezing all the jammy cloves out of their skins. It will be too hot to handle initially, but you can let it cool on the side until you're able to.
6. Add the coconut milk and enough stock to cover the roasted vegetables.
7. Bring the soup to a boil, then reduce to a simmer for 30 minutes.
8. Blend with an immersion blender or in a blender until smooth, then taste and adjust the seasoning.
9. To make the salsa, combine all the ingredients in a small bowl.
10. Serve the soup in bowls and top with the salsa. I like to add some chili oil too, for an extra kick, and scoop it all up with some toasted bread.

Salt & Vinegar Potato Soup

If you have made my pierogi recipe from the Dinner section of this book, you will know that it is a time-consuming, yet rewarding endeavor. I don't always have the time to hand-make dumplings, but I often crave pierogi, and when I do, I make this soup. It has all the flavors of a pierogi but takes a fraction of the time and is delivered in a warming broth that feels more appropriate for lunchtime.

Serves 6–8

2¼ lb baby potatoes
3 tbsp butter
1 tbsp olive oil
3 large white onions, diced
sea salt and black pepper
4 cups vegetable stock
1 tbsp white wine vinegar
a medium bunch of dill,
    roughly chopped
7 oz sauerkraut
⅔ cup sour cream
a medium bunch of chives,
    finely chopped

1. Boil the potatoes in well-salted water until tender, around 20 minutes depending on the size of your potatoes. They are cooked when a knife slips easily through them.
2. In a large heavy-bottomed pan over medium heat, melt the butter with the olive oil and add the onions, 1 teaspoon of salt, and ½ teaspoon of black pepper.
3. Cook the onions for at least 20 minutes and anywhere up to 40 minutes, so they get jammy and caramelized.
4. Remove a quarter of the onions from the pan and reserve them for topping later.
5. Add the stock, vinegar, and all the potatoes to the pan. With a potato masher, or the back of a wooden spoon, break up the potatoes to release some of their fluffy interior—this will help to thicken up the soup.
6. Continue to simmer for 15 minutes, to allow some of the liquid to reduce and thicken.
7. Stir in all the chopped dill and half the sauerkraut.
8. Serve in bowls, topped with a dollop of sour cream, a sprinkle of chives, the rest of the sauerkraut, the reserved caramelized onions, and more black pepper.

Bee's Potato Flatbreads

This is another classic recipe from my former housemate Bee; she always makes these flatbreads to accompany her dal and I always eat too many of them because I can't help myself. They are the fluffiest, easiest, and most pleasing flatbreads to make, and I can't recommend them enough. I also particularly like them the next day, toasted and buttered with a jammy soft-boiled egg for breakfast. They freeze incredibly well, so it's always worth making the full batch and freezing any you can't finish.

Makes 8 large flatbreads, or 12 baby ones

4 large potatoes
2 cups + 2½ tbsp bread flour, plus extra
    for dusting
1 tsp sea salt
1 tsp nigella seeds
butter of your choice, for serving

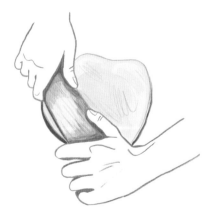

1. Boil the potatoes, skin on, for 30-40 minutes, or until tender and cooked through.
2. In a large bowl, mash the potatoes thoroughly. You can keep the skins—we like to do it this way to keep things simple and easy, but also because it adds a lovely texture to the finished flatbreads.
3. Once the potatoes have stopped steaming and are cool enough to handle, but still warm, add the flour, salt, and nigella seeds and mix into a dough. You can start with a spoon and then move on to kneading by hand.
4. Transfer the dough to a clean work surface. Knead into a smooth dough, adding more flour if it feels sticky. You are aiming for a supple, smooth dough.
5. Roll into a cylindrical shape and cut into 8 equal discs.
6. Take a disc of dough, flour each side, then flatten with your hands into a round flatbread roughly the thickness of a quarter.
7. Heat a large frying pan over medium heat and cook each flatbread for 5-8 minutes, or until the dough is no longer raw and the flatbread has charred in places, flipping to ensure an even color on both sides. There is no need for oil when cooking, the hot dry pan is perfect.
8. Serve with butter, dipped into dal, curry, stew or even with boiled eggs as a dreamy breakfast.

Pier's Shrimp & Green Onion Pancakes

When I moved into the warehouse, I was hot on the heels of a big breakup. I collapsed at the kitchen table, broken and ravenous. My housemate Pier, whom I didn't know at all at the time, was making shrimp and green onion pancakes. Just as I sat down at the table, he wordlessly placed a perfect pancake in front of me. I didn't know how hungry I was until I took the first bite of that perfect pancake. I was hungry for food, but more than that, I was hungry for community, for friendship, and to be nourished by those around me. From that moment forward Pier and I have been firm friends. When I think of home, I think of Pier standing by the stove, tending to a pot of something delicious, always primed to feed whoever walks through the door—whether they are hungry or not, he is ready. This pancake is still my favorite thing that Pier makes and I implore you to make it at your earliest convenience—it's a winner!

Makes 6 large pancakes

For the pancakes:

4 cups all-purpose flour

1 tsp white pepper

2 tsp sea salt

6 eggs

2 cups water

12 green onions, cut into thirds and then each third halved lengthwise, reserving a handful of the green tops for the sauce

5 large garlic cloves, thinly sliced

vegetable oil, for frying

10 oz peeled shrimp, butterflied and deveined

1. In a large bowl, whisk together the flour, white pepper, and salt.
2. Add the eggs and water and whisk until smooth.
3. Fold in the prepared green onions and garlic.
4. Set a medium frying pan over medium-high heat and add 3 tablespoons of vegetable oil.
5. Once the oil is hot, add a ladle of the pancake batter, enough to cover the bottom of the pan, tilting and encouraging the batter to the edges to make a big circular pancake, around ⅜ inch thick. This will be different for everyone depending on what size of pan you use, but you want a good layer of batter covering the bottom of the pan so it can puff up and cradle the shrimp.
6. Immediately add one-sixth of the shrimp (roughly 5), pushing them into the batter, spacing them so they are evenly dispersed throughout the pancake.
7. Cook on this side for around 3 minutes, until the underside is crisp, has started to brown, and the shrimp have started to turn pink.

(recipe continues)

For the sauce:

⅓ of the green onion tops, finely sliced

7½ tbsp soy sauce

2½ tbsp rice vinegar

2 tbsp Asian sesame sauce (or tahini)

1 tbsp sugar

1 tbsp gochujang paste

1 tbsp toasted sesame seeds

For serving:

chili oil, for serving (optional)

8. Carefully flip the pancake and cook on the other side for approximately 1 minute, until the shrimp are cooked and there isn't any raw batter left.

9. Turn out onto a plate and continue until all the batter has been used up. The first pancake will always be the worst—you will get better the more you make, learning how long they need on each side and when to flip. You'll need to top up the oil in the pan as you go.

10. To make the sauce, put all the ingredients into a bowl and whisk to combine.

11. Serve each pancake drizzled with the sauce and perhaps some chili oil too.

Erbazzone Reggiano

I knew for a long time that I didn't want to be in London for my thirtieth birthday. Luckily, my housemate Virginia and her family very generously offered to host the warehouse at their home in Reggio Emilia, Italy. So in mid-April all of us flew out to Bologna, then drove an hour out to her little village near Correggio. This part of Italy is a cook's DREAM, being the home to Parmigiano-Reggiano, aceto balsamico, Lambrusco, Prosciutto di Parma, and, of course, Ferrari. We spent the weekend wandering the beautiful streets, eating, drinking, and shopping for, you guessed it, more food—chief among them was erbazzone. This pastry-encased snack is extremely specific to the surrounding area of Reggio Emilia—you cannot find it anywhere else in the country—and showcases their legendary local cheese, Parmigiano-Reggiano. It traditionally uses pork fat in the pastry, to give it a distinctive flavor and flaky texture. It's simply delicious, the perfect snack, and available at pretty much every café and bar you walk into in the area. This recipe uses butter instead of pork fat, and while it's not traditional, it's certainly a snack.

Serves 6 generously

For the pastry:

1½ cups / 200g bread flour, plus extra for dusting

a pinch of salt

3 tbsp / 40g unsalted butter, chilled and cubed

⅓ cup + 2 tbsp / 100ml warm water

1 egg, beaten, for egg wash

For the filling:

1 large white onion, thinly sliced

4½ tbsp / 60g unsalted butter

black pepper

2 lb / 1kg frozen chopped spinach, thawed and squeezed dry

3 cups / 150g finely grated Parmesan (use another hard cheese to keep this recipe V)

sea salt

1. Preheat the oven to 400°F. Grease a 9 × 13-inch sheet pan and line with parchment paper.
2. Whisk together the flour and salt, then rub in the butter until it resembles wet sand.
3. Gradually add the warm water, mixing until a shaggy dough forms.
4. Knead until smooth, then wrap the dough in plastic wrap and rest in the fridge for 30 minutes.
5. Meanwhile, make the filling: sauté the onion in the butter until it is soft and jammy.
6. Season with a good grind of black pepper and take off the heat. We aren't adding any salt yet, as the Parmesan is very salty.
7. In a mixing bowl, combine the onion, spinach, and Parmesan. Taste the mix and adjust for seasoning, adding a little salt if necessary.
8. Take the pastry out of the fridge and cut it in half.
9. On a lightly floured surface, roll one half out for the base, slightly larger than the pan so that the pastry hangs over the edge, leaving a ½-inch border all around. Add the

filling in a single even layer, then roll out the other half of dough and place on top.

10. Seal the edges tightly, by pinching the two pieces of dough together, then prick the top of the pastry a few times to allow steam to escape in the oven.

11. Bake for 20 minutes, then egg wash the top and bake again for another 10 minutes, or until golden brown and crisp on the bottom.

Potato, Mozzarella & Rosemary Galette

Galettes are often sweet, freeform pastry pies, but my favorite way to make them is with savory fillings. This one takes all the comforting savory elements—creamy, fatty, salty, and crisp—while utilizing one of my favorite pizza topping combos: potato and rosemary. You can make the pastry and the shallot mix up to five days ahead, making this a very speedy assembly job on the day you want to eat it. Or you can do it all in one day; just allow an hour for chilling the pastry.

Serves 6–8

For the pastry:

1 cup + 2½ tbsp / 115g whole-grain spelt flour, plus extra for dusting

¾ cup + 1½ tbsp / 115g bread flour

1 tsp sea salt

1 cup (2 sticks) / 230g cold unsalted butter, cubed

⅓ cup / 80g ice water

2 tsp fine semolina

1 egg, beaten, for egg wash

For the filling:

14 oz / 400g shallots, thinly sliced

3 tbsp olive oil

3–4 new potatoes

sea salt and black pepper

4 sprigs of rosemary, leaves picked and finely chopped

1 oz / 25g Parmesan (use another hard cheese to keep this recipe V)

9 oz / 250g mozzarella, roughly torn into pieces

1. To make the pastry, whisk together the spelt flour, bread flour, and salt, then rub in the butter. Start by flattening each cube of butter and then rubbing in until it is well incorporated, but a few chunky pieces of butter still remain—this helps to keep the pastry flaky.

2. Next, work the ice water in bit by bit, with a knife and using a cutting motion, until a dough begins to form.

3. Tip the pastry mix out onto a floured work surface and bring it together into a dough, adding a little more water if necessary, or a spot of either flour if it feels too dry.

4. Once you have a cohesive dough, roll it out into a long rectangle. Fold it into thirds, like a letter. Roll it out into a rectangle again and repeat the folding and rolling twice more.

5. Shape the dough into a round, wrap tightly in plastic wrap, and chill in the fridge for at least 1 hour.

6. Meanwhile, sauté the shallots in 2 tablespoons of the olive oil for 30 minutes, until they are completely cooked down and caramelized. Do this over medium heat so they don't catch and crisp up—you want them to still be almost translucent and jammy in consistency.

7. Prep the potatoes by slicing them into rounds as thinly as possible; you can do this on a mandoline with ease, or using a sharp knife with a little concentration. Mix the potato slices with the remaining tablespoon of olive oil, 1 teaspoon of salt, ½ teaspoon of pepper, and the chopped rosemary.

8. When you are ready to assemble the tart, preheat the oven to 425°F and line a sheet pan with parchment paper.

(recipe continues)

9. Take the pastry out of the fridge and allow it to come to room temperature for 10 minutes. Then roll out on a floured work surface into a large round, about 2 inches bigger than a dinner plate, and the thickness of a quarter. Take the dinner plate and gently press it face down in the center of the pastry round, creating a circle indent for you to work within.

10. Transfer the pastry to the lined sheet pan and sprinkled with the semolina (this helps the pastry stay crisp, so you don't have a soggy bottom!).

11. Spread the jammy shallots on the pastry first, staying within the circle, then grate the Parmesan directly on top.

12. Next, layer half the potato slices, making sure to separate them, then add the mozzarella in an even layer, finishing with the rest of the potato slices, a good grind of black pepper, and a sprinkle of sea salt.

13. Fold the edges of the pastry around the filling, making little pleats as you go.

14. Brush the beaten egg over all the visible pastry, then bake for 35 minutes, until the pastry is golden brown and the filling is bubbling and crisping up.

15. Let cool on the pan for 10 minutes, then transfer to a large board, slice while still warm, and serve.

Sourdough Focaccia, Three Ways

This bread is a *three-day mission*, but my god, it's worth it. If you have made lots of sourdough before you will be familiar with stretching, folding, and making a levain. If this is your first foray into sourdough, I actually think it is a great place to start—the shaping is almost nonexistent, so it's a good way to come to grips with the method before you tackle a banneton-shaped loaf, which requires skilled shaping, scoring, and baking in a cast-iron pot. If you haven't made sourdough since the dark days of 2020 but you still have a starter sitting at the back of your fridge, I would recommend taking it out and feeding it once a day for a few days before you attempt this loaf, to ensure you have a lively, healthy starter to work with. This is a great recipe to get back to sourdough baking with. We serve it at every single one of our supper clubs and it has become somewhat famous as a result.

Makes 1 large loaf

For the levain:
25g starter, recently fed
½ cup / 50g bread flour
¼ cup / 50ml warm water

For the dough:
3½ cups + 3 tbsp / 500g bread flour
1¾ cups / 425g warm water
2 tsp sea salt
⅔ cup / 150ml good-quality extra-virgin olive oil

1. Day one: Make the levain by mixing the starter, bread flour, and water. Cover and leave out at room temperature overnight.
2. Day two: Autolyse—premix—the bread flour thoroughly with the warm water, until there are no dry spots of flour remaining, then leave covered at room temperature for 3 hours.
3. Scoop 100g of the levain on top of the dough, and with a wet hand, scrunch the levain into the dough until it is evenly incorporated. Leave covered at room temperature for 1 hour.
4. With a wet hand, scrunch the sea salt through the dough until evenly incorporated.
5. For the next 2 hours, stretch and fold the dough every 30 minutes, leaving it covered at room temperature in between folds.
6. I like to have my dough in a rectangular airtight box, big enough to hold double the size of the dough, and to do all the stretching and folding in this container. This ensures the dough is already in a rough rectangular shape for baking. I use the coil folding method, which is where you lift one end of the dough until it folds in on itself and keep

(recipe continues)

Classico:

extra-virgin olive oil

flaky sea salt

Potato & rosemary:

1 medium potato, sliced into very
    thin rounds

sea salt

3 sprigs of rosemary, leaves picked

extra-virgin olive oil

black pepper

Tomato:

3 tbsp passata (or tomato puree)

extra-virgin olive oil

sea salt

doing so until the dough has been coiled into a log, not dissimilar to the shape of a jelly-roll.

7. After 2 hours, add the olive oil and continue coil folding every 30 minutes for another 2 hours. It will be slippery and hard to handle, but persevere—as long as you are adding tension to the dough you will be fine. This process is rippling the oil through the dough.

8. When 4 hours have passed, from the beginning of your coil folds, it's time to transfer the dough to a 9 × 13-inch sheet pan lined with parchment paper. To do this, I like to lift my dough onto the pan and then do a few more coil folds to tuck it into the pan nicely. You can pour any excess oil left in the container over the dough at this point.

9. Leave the dough out at room temperature until it's visibly bubbly; this can take between 30 minutes and 2 hours, depending on the temperature of your kitchen and the weather, so keep an eye on the dough and when it looks jiggly and bubbly, pop it into the fridge.

10. Store in the fridge overnight, trying not to let anything touch the top of the dough as it will stick and rip the dough when you remove it.

11. Day three: preheat the oven to 500°F, with a heavy sheet pan or baking stone on the middle rack.

12. Take the focaccia out of the fridge and let it sit at room temperature while the oven heats up. When you are ready to bake, dimple the dough with oiled hands, pressing right to the bottom of the pan, then add your chosen toppings, and do another light dimple.

13. Bake for 25 to 30 minutes in the middle of the oven, until cooked through and a deep golden brown. Let the focaccia cool completely in the pan, then slice and enjoy.

Classico:

1. Add a good drizzle of extra-virgin olive oil and a sprinkle of flaky salt.

Potato & rosemary:

1. Prepare the potato topping the day before making by soaking the potato slices in water with 1 teaspoon of salt overnight in the fridge.

2. Take the potato slices, drain and dry thoroughly, then toss with the rosemary, a little olive oil, and salt and pepper, until all the pieces are well coated.
3. After dimpling the dough, add the potato, pressing the slices into the dough.

Tomato:
1. Before dimpling the dough, spread the passata out evenly and then dimple, pushing right to the bottom of the pan.
2. Finish with another drizzle of oil and a sprinkle of sea salt.

In for Dinner

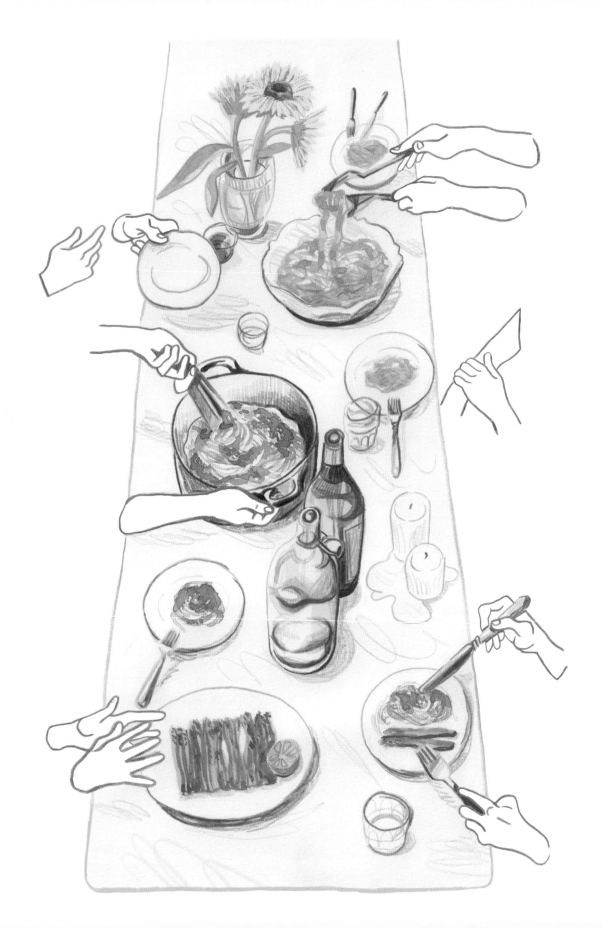

In for Dinner

Now, there are a lot of names for this meal in the UK. I grew up calling it tea, as did my parents and their parents before them. I can imagine this being confusing to anyone not from the UK, when we also have afternoon tea, which refers to a late-afternoon cup of tea, sandwiches, scones, and cake. At my school, the meal in the middle of the day was referred to as dinner, with dinner ladies serving our food. So, we had breakfast, dinner at school, and tea when we got home. Then "supper" is a word my Grandma Pat used for her cup of tea and "something sweet" that she had every night before bed. However, I am aware that some people would call the evening meal supper as well. We run a supper club, which is really a dinner party. It's all very confusing and I have recently learned that in the UK, the name that you call the evening meal is determined by class. Commonly the working class call it tea and the middle to upper class call it dinner or supper. The distinction being that you refer to your largest meal of the day as dinner, and in many working-class communities this would have been the meal in the middle of the day, perhaps due to labor-intensive jobs. So while this chapter was originally titled "supper," in reference to our supper clubs, I have changed it to dinner, as in the warehouse the person cooking asks every day, "Who's in for dinner?"

Whatever you call this meal, it is the one that brings the most people together in our house, and in most homes, too—whether that is just a collection of our housemates or a bigger group of friends, there is always something on offer in the evening, for whoever wants it. My dad comes to London for work every other week, and he makes a point of booking dinner at the warehouse at least once a month. On those occasions my sister Grace usually joins us, and if cousin Jake is around, then it's a given he will be there too. By the time all the boyfriends who don't live with us have decided to join, we can easily have a dozen people round the table. I love evenings like this, I live for them. I am at my happiest serving out twelve glossy plates of pasta, lighting candles, and pouring wine for my friends, a crumble bub-

bling away in the oven. I have been known to get carried away and invite too many people, but we always make it work—whether we are perching on each other's knees, eating with chopsticks for lack of forks or out of Tupperware for lack of plates, it is always a complete joy.

In this chapter you will find our staple warehouse dinners, some classic childhood teatime moments, and a few of the recipes from our supper clubs too. If I persuade you to do one thing after reading this book, please let it be to cook one of these dinners for your housemates, friends, family, neighbors—anyone! They are so much more delicious eaten with others, and the more you do it, the easier, more enjoyable, and addictive it gets.

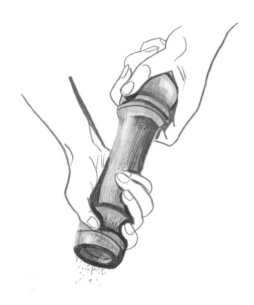

Simple weekday dinners: the quick and easy meals soon to be in your weekly rotation

- Pantry Pasta
- Pantry Ramen
- Pasta al Pomodoro
- Mushroom Pasta
- Pesto Pasta & Green Beans
- Spaghetti Puttanesca
- Sticky Eggplant Rice
- Okonomiyaki
- Brothy Fregola & Tomatoes
- Citrus Mackerel Spaghetti with Pangrattato
- Maple-Glazed Tofu & Garlic Fried Rice
- A Spring Pea Risotto
- Baked Beans
- Cheese Knödel
- Bee's Flammkuchen

Small plates: destined for friends—pick a few and put them together for a feast
- Sticky Sweet Potatoes, Tahini & Pickled Red Chile
- Roasted Asparagus, Lemon & Olive Oil
- The Hummus Plate
- Jammy Shallot Harissa Bulgur
- Harissa Honey Roasted Carrots, Tahini Yogurt & Sesame Seeds
- Hasselback Potatoes, Miso Almond Sauce, Massaged Kale & Lemon Dressing
- Sesame Spinach
- Last of the Summer Tomatoes, Roasted Squash & Brown Butter Hazelnuts
- Minted Garden Peas, Fava Beans & Sizzled Green Onions over Whipped Lemony Ricotta

Hosting: meals for big groups, gatherings, and special occasions
- A Summer Feast
- Black Bean Chili & Charred Corn Salsa
- Cacio e Pepe
- Caponata, Fried Bread & Couscous
- Gnocchi alla Sorrentina
- Macaroni Cheese
- Potato & Pineapple Massaman Curry
- Roasted Squash, Browned Butter, Crispy Sage, Hazelnuts & Wilted Lacinato Kale
- Sri Lankan Dal with Coconut Sambal

A weekend project: something to dedicate an afternoon or more to, a dinner to savor
- Mezze Feast
- Conchigliette with Porcini Mushroom Ragù
- Orecchiette Pasta e Ceci
- Pierogi
- The Best Pizza You'll Make at Home
- Tomato, Spinach & Ricotta Lasagna
- Ramps Tagliatelle, Butter & Parmesan

Pantry Pasta

Call it what you want, I think we all have a version of this pasta. My housemate Wojciech often announces he is "just gonna make a quick pasta," and when he does my heart soars: his version is always heavy on the garlic, anchovies, capers, and olives, and I love him for it. The key here is making the most of what you have in the pantry, so that at all times you can whip up a delicious bowl of pasta, should the need arise. Below is just one delicious version, but other worthy components include marinated artichokes, tomato paste, confit tomatoes, confit garlic, jarred peppers, canned beans, bread crumbs, and of course other canned fish.

Serves 6

7 tbsp olive oil, plus extra for drizzling
6 garlic cloves, thinly sliced
1 tsp sea salt
½ tsp black pepper
1 tin of anchovy fillets (use 1 tbsp of white miso to keep this recipe V)
zest and juice of 2 lemons
3 tbsp capers, roughly chopped
3 tbsp olives, roughly chopped
1 tsp chile flakes (or chili crisp oil)
1 lb pasta (whatever you have, it seriously works with everything. Use gluten-free pasta to keep this recipe GF)
a large bunch of flat-leaf parsley (or other soft herbs such as chives, basil, or dill)
3½ oz Parmesan, finely grated (or use another hard cheese to keep this recipe V)

1. Bring a large saucepan of salted water to a boil.
2. Heat the olive oil in a heavy-bottomed pan, then add the garlic, salt, and pepper and cook for 5 minutes, just until the garlic starts to brown.
3. Add the anchovies (or miso), lemon zest and juice, capers, olives, and chile flakes. Stir to combine and cook for 10 minutes to allow the anchovies to melt and everything to soften.
4. Cook the pasta in the salted water until just under al dente.
5. Scoop the pasta out of its cooking water and add to the garlic mix along with a ladle of pasta water, stirring well to combine. This should emulsify the garlic paste into a more saucy mix.
6. Keep cooking until the pasta reaches al dente, adding more pasta water if necessary.
7. When you are ready to serve, stir in all the parsley and half the Parmesan, adding more pasta water if you want to loosen it up.
8. Serve topped with the rest of the Parmesan and a drizzle of olive oil, maybe some more chile flakes for good measure.

Pantry Ramen

I love ramen with all my soul, and often crave it in the dead of winter, when we are all run down and in need of a quick but nourishing meal. Enter the pantry ramen: this recipe takes advantage of the heroic instant noodle, but doesn't compromise on flavor; it is made out of the ingredients in your pantry and can be on the table in under 10 minutes. Ramen has five basic components: broth, tare (sauce), noodles, toppings, and oil. Stock up on the ingredients from your local Asian store; they will last you a good couple of months. You make this recipe mostly in the bowl you will eat it from, so I have written it to make one bowl, but it can be easily scaled.

Serves 1

For the tare (sauce):
1 tbsp white miso
1 tbsp Asian sesame paste (you can
    substitute tahini or peanut butter)
1 garlic clove, finely grated
1 tsp sesame oil
1 tsp soy sauce
1 tsp rice vinegar (or whichever vinegar
    you have on hand)
1 tbsp toasted sesame seeds

For the noodles:
1 pack of your favorite instant noodles
    (I go for the most neutral flavor so
    that the sauce can really shine)
3½ oz fried tofu puffs (or another
    protein of your choice)

For the toppings:
1 green onion, finely chopped
1 jammy egg (or a marinated egg if you
    have one; see page 36)
1 tsp black sesame seeds
your favorite chili crisp oil

1. In a deep bowl, whisk together all the tare ingredients.
2. Cook the instant noodles according to the packet instructions, with their seasoning. Add the tofu puffs to the pan at the same time, to heat while the noodles cook. They will soak up a good amount of the broth too, which is ideal.
3. Thin out the sauce in the bowl with some of the noodle broth, to your desired consistency. Add the noodles and tofu to the bowl.
4. Top with the green onion, boiled egg, black sesame seeds, and chili crisp oil (for me it's the peanut and chili oil from Lao Gan Ma).

Pasta al Pomodoro

I believe everyone should have a good tomato pasta recipe up their sleeve. It's the most simple of staples, but it's surprisingly easy to get wrong, and there are a few things you should be doing to make sure it's as delicious as possible. The quality of your ingredients here is key—there are so few that you want them to all be the best quality so they can really sing. I encourage you to buy the best tomatoes you can afford. I like to use Mutti Polpa—I prefer my sauce to be smooth and not have lots of lumps of tomato, so these are perfect. The other thing that will really make a difference is great olive oil and good-quality pasta. No one has bags of money to spare right now, but if you can spare a little extra for these ingredients, I promise you will taste the difference (not sponsored by Sainsbury's).

Serves 6

1 whole head of garlic (or 10–15 cloves)
7 tbsp olive oil
a small bunch of basil, leaves and
    stems separated, plus a few more
    for serving
sea salt and black pepper
2 tsp sugar, plus extra as needed
2 tbsp tomato paste
3 (14 oz) cans finely chopped tomatoes
1 lb spaghetti (use gluten-free spaghetti
    to keep this recipe GF)
grated Parmesan, for serving (omit to
    keep this recipe vegan)

1. Peel all the garlic cloves and slice them as thinly as possible—just like that prison scene in the movie *Goodfellas*.
2. Place a large pot over medium heat and fry the garlic in the olive oil for a few minutes. Finely chop the basil stems and add these to the garlic, with a pinch of salt and a good grind of black pepper. Keep frying until the garlic is just about to color.
3. Add the sugar and tomato paste and keep cooking until it is broken down and has gone from bright red to a deeper color.
4. Add all the canned tomatoes, rinsing out the cans with a little water and adding this tomatoey liquid to the pan as well.
5. Bring to a boil, then reduce to a simmer for 30 minutes, stirring occasionally.
6. Taste the sauce for seasoning and add more salt, pepper, or sugar to taste. Then wilt the basil leaves into the sauce, stirring until well combined.
7. When you are happy with the sauce and it has reduced by around a quarter, to a thicker consistency, cook the pasta in heavily salted water until al dente.
8. Drain the pasta and add the sauce. Toss until the pasta is well coated in the glossy sauce and serve immediately with a mountain of grated Parmesan, and more salt and pepper.

Mushroom Pasta

This is my version of another Kellett family classic that we ate for dinner a lot as children. I was never much of a fan of this meal growing up, and I think that was down to the addition of heavy cream, which I still find a bit much in savory food. In my version I opt for crème fraîche, which feels a little more savory and less sickly sweet. I've also added a bunch of herbs and some lemon juice that would never be found in the original, so I very much took a family classic and ran with it here. This is a great meal to make on a mediocre Wednesday to brighten up your week and your table.

Serves 6

½ cup + 2 tbsp unsalted butter
2¼ lb mixed mushrooms, roughly
   chopped
black pepper
1 tbsp olive oil
1¼ cups white wine
1 tsp sea salt
1⅓ cups crème fraîche
juice of 1 lemon
a small bunch each of flat-leaf parsley
   and dill, finely chopped
5 oz grated Parmesan, plus extra
   for serving (use another hard cheese
   to keep this recipe V)
1 lb penne pasta (use gluten-free pasta
   to keep this recipe GF)
zest of 1 lemon, for serving

1. In a large saucepan, melt the butter over medium-high heat. Once fully melted, add all the mushrooms, 1 teaspoon of pepper, and the olive oil and stir until well combined.
2. Cook the mushrooms like this over high heat for around 10 minutes, until cooked down and starting to color.
3. Add the white wine and salt, bring to a boil, then simmer until the wine has reduced by half.
4. Add the crème fraîche, lemon juice, herbs, and Parmesan, and stir until the cheese is melted and everything is well combined, allowing the sauce to simmer while you cook the pasta.
5. Cook the penne until al dente in well-salted water. Drain and then combine with the sauce.
6. Serve with the lemon zest, more Parmesan, and a good grind of black pepper.

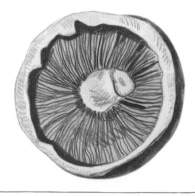

Pesto Pasta & Green Beans

Pesto pasta remains one of my favorite, most nostalgic meals of all time. Fresh homemade pesto is pretty unbeatable, and I can hand on heart say it's my favorite pasta sauce. There, I've said it. This one uses almond flour, which originally was born out of frugality. Pine nuts have recently become completely unaffordable for me—almonds are a bit cheaper, but almond flour is cheaper still. Now I always choose to use almond flour, as it is not only cheaper but far less hassle than blending whole nuts, and it lends a delicious sweetness to the pesto, which I have grown to adore.

Serves 6

a small bunch of basil
a small bunch of flat-leaf parsley
1 cup olive oil, plus extra as needed
3½ oz grated Parmesan, plus extra
    for topping
1 garlic clove
sea salt and black pepper
¾ cup + 2 tbsp almond flour
1 lb casarecce, or another long tubular
    pasta (use gluten-free pasta to keep
    this recipe GF)
7 oz French green beans

1. Blend the basil, parsley, olive oil, Parmesan, garlic, and 1 teaspoon each of salt and pepper in a blender until smooth.
2. Transfer to a bowl and stir in the almond flour. If the mixture looks dry, add a little more olive oil—it should be more of a sauce than a paste.
3. Bring a large saucepan of salted water to a boil and cook the pasta until al dente, adding the green beans 3 minutes before the end of the cooking time, unless they are super thick, in which case add them a minute or two sooner.
4. Drain the pasta and beans, then toss with the pesto.
5. Serve topped with more Parmesan, salt, and pepper.

Spaghetti Puttanesca

Forever "Slut's Spaghetti" to me—thank you, Nigella. This is my take on a classic; it brings together everything I love, all the salty-sour ingredients with a silky sauce and the sexiest of pasta shapes. Make it for your lover, make it for yourself, and whatever you do, make sure you enjoy yourself while eating it.

Serves 6

2 tbsp olive oil
8 garlic cloves, crushed
½ red onion, thinly sliced
a small bunch of flat-leaf parsley, stems finely chopped, leaves reserved
1 tin of anchovy fillets, drained
1 tsp chile flakes
2 tbsp tomato paste
sea salt and black pepper
1 (14 oz) can whole peeled tomatoes
2 cups passata (or tomato puree)
3 tbsp capers
3½ oz (about ⅔ cup) of your favorite olives, roughly chopped
1 tsp sugar
1 lb spaghetti (use gluten-free spaghetti to keep this recipe GF)
grated Parmesan, for topping

1. Heat the olive oil in a heavy-bottomed pan, then add the garlic, onion, and parsley stems and cook for 2–3 minutes.
2. Next add the anchovies, chile flakes, tomato paste, and a good pinch of salt and pepper, stir and continue to cook for a few minutes.
3. Add the canned tomatoes, passata, capers, olives, and sugar, bring to a boil, then lower to a simmer.
4. Cook the spaghetti in a saucepan of well-salted water until al dente.
5. Drain the pasta and combine with the sauce.
6. Serve immediately, topped with the parsley leaves and a little Parmesan.

Sticky Eggplant Rice

When I want a comforting, speedy dinner and I don't feel like pasta, I make this eggplant rice. It's so easy and delivers a deep umami flavor that makes me feel beyond cozy. It's naturally free of most allergens and is suitable for vegan, gluten-free, and nut-free friends, so this is a great choice if you have lots of dietary requirements to cater to. Perfect as a light lunch for six, a more filling meal for four, or as meal prep for your weekday lunches.

Serves 4–6

For the rice:

2½ cups sticky rice (Southeast Asian glutinous rice)

1 cup + 3 tbsp water

1 (13.5 oz) can coconut milk

For the eggplant:

3 large eggplants, halved lengthwise to make 6 halves

3 garlic cloves, crushed

1½ tbsp white miso

1½ tbsp honey (or maple syrup)

2 tbsp soy sauce (or use tamari to keep this recipe GF)

To serve:

6 green onions, thinly sliced

chili crisp oil

toasted sesame seeds

1. Preheat the oven to 400°F.
2. Soak the rice for 30 minutes in enough cold water to cover.
3. For the eggplant, take each half and score the flesh in a crisscross action all over, being careful not to pierce the skin on the underside.
4. Place the eggplant halves side by side on a foil-lined sheet pan—this will catch any of the sticky marinade that ends up on the bottom of the pan and will make cleaning a lot easier!
5. Whisk together the garlic, miso, honey, and soy sauce and brush this over each eggplant half. Pour any remaining liquid equally over the eggplants.
6. Bake in the oven for 35 minutes, basting with the marinade halfway through.
7. Meanwhile, drain the rice and rinse in a bowl until the water runs clear, at least three times.
8. Bring the water and coconut milk to a boil in a medium saucepan, with a tight-fitting lid. Add the rice, reduce the heat to a low simmer, fit the lid on the pan, and cook over low heat for 20 minutes. Remove the pan from the heat but keep the lid on tightly for another 15 minutes—no peeking! The steam is doing the last bit of cooking work for the rice here, so don't be tempted to have a look until the time is up.
9. Serve the rice with the eggplants and top with the green onions, chili crisp oil, and sesame seeds.

Okonomiyaki

This is another recipe my housemate Bee introduced me to—she is known to get a hankering for one of these pancakes, decisively go to the store for the ingredients, then whip up some fat okonomiyaki for the warehouse, with crispy bacon, Kewpie mayo, and hoisin sauce. It's a very filling, comforting meal, and one that I had always been a little intimidated by. I learned quickly that not only is it delicious, but it is very simple and quick to whip up.

Makes 6 large pancakes

For the pancakes:
6 eggs
1½ cups all-purpose flour
¾ cup + 1½ tbsp milk
1 tsp sea salt
1 tsp baking powder
1 tsp vegetable oil, plus extra for frying
1 tsp soy sauce
1 Chinese napa cabbage or white Savoy cabbage (about 1 lb, thinly sliced)
a bunch of green onions, thinly sliced, white part and green tops separated

For the sauce:
5 tbsp hoisin sauce
2 tbsp soy sauce

For the toppings:
Kewpie mayo
chili crisp oil
the saved green onion tops
crispy seaweed
toasted sesame seeds

1. Preheat the oven to its lowest setting; you'll use it later to keep the pancakes warm while you cook them one by one.
2. In a large bowl, whisk together the eggs, flour, milk, salt, baking powder, vegetable oil, and soy sauce.
3. Fold the thinly sliced cabbage and white part of the green onions into the mix until well combined.
4. Heat a large frying pan over medium-high heat, then drizzle a little vegetable oil in the pan, tipping the pan to spread it evenly, to cover the bottom. Add a ladle of batter to the pan and allow to cook for 7–8 minutes.
5. Loosen the edges of the pancake once it is fully set on the bottom side, give it a jiggle in the pan, then flip the pancake and cook on the other side for 3–5 minutes until evenly cooked all the way through. You can check by inserting a skewer in the middle—if it comes out clean it's cooked. You'll get a sense of how long they take after a few tries. The pancake should be around ⅜ inch thick and golden brown on both sides.
6. Keep the pancakes warm in the oven while you cook the rest.
7. To make the sauce, whisk together the hoisin and soy sauces.
8. Top each pancake with a drizzle of Kewpie mayo, the hoisin-soy sauce, chili crisp oil, a sprinkle of the green onion tops, crispy seaweed, and toasted sesame seeds.
9. You can keep the batter in the fridge for up to 3 days, so if you don't want to make a full batch in one go you don't have to.

Brothy Fregola & Tomatoes

There's something very comforting to me about a meal you can eat with a spoon, maybe even a little reminiscent of nursery food. This tiny pasta shape is one of my favorites for this very reason; it is perfectly scoopable and sits very happily in a broth or soup. On a certain brand of gray day, a bowl of this brothy fregola really hits the spot. It's simple, clean, quick, and easy. If you aren't familiar with this pasta shape, then it is my honor to introduce you to the chicest of pastas—if you struggle to find it at the store, orzo will substitute well, just make sure to adjust the cooking time according to the package instructions.

Serves 6

1 lb fregola (or orzo)
3 tbsp olive oil
5 banana shallots, thinly sliced
sea salt and black pepper
1 lb 5 oz (about 4 cups) cherry tomatoes
a pinch of chile flakes
1 cup white wine
3 cups vegetable stock
2 oz Parmesan, finely grated (omit to keep this recipe vegan)
a few knobs of butter (use plant-based butter to keep this recipe vegan)

1. Cook the fregola in heavily salted water until al dente, about 7 minutes. Reserve a mug (roughly ¾ cup) of the pasta water, then thoroughly drain.
2. Heat the olive oil in a heavy-bottomed pan and sauté the shallots with 1 teaspoon of salt and ½ teaspoon of pepper until softened, about 15 minutes.
3. Add the cherry tomatoes and chile flakes and continue cooking until the tomatoes start to blister and burst.
4. Add the white wine and vegetable stock, bring to a boil, then lower to a simmer for 20 minutes.
5. Put the fregola into the tomato mixture and stir to combine, tasting for seasoning. Add more salt and pepper if needed.
6. Loosen with a splash of the reserved pasta water, until you reach your desired brothyness.
7. Ladle into bowls and top with the grated Parmesan, a knob of butter, and more salt and pepper.

Citrus Mackerel Spaghetti with Pangrattato

This recipe was born, like the best of them, out of necessity. While living with my first boyfriend in my early twenties, we existed almost exclusively on BLTs and a version of this pasta. Tinned fish and dried pasta were affordable, and this recipe became a staple dinner. It's for the cash poor and the time poor, yet it's serving big-time flavor. It's made up of pantry staples and will be on the table in less than half an hour.

Serves 6

7 slices of stale bread
¼ cup extra-virgin olive oil, plus extra as needed
1 garlic clove, minced
1 lb spaghetti
4 (4.4 oz) tins of mackerel in olive oil, drained and broken up
1 (6 oz) jar of capers, drained and finely chopped
2 tsp chile flakes
zest and juice of 3 lemons
a large bunch of flat-leaf parsley, leaves and stems finely chopped
sea salt and black pepper

1. First make the pangrattato by blitzing the bread into bread crumbs in a food processor.
2. In a frying pan, over medium heat, heat a tablespoon of the olive oil and fry the bread crumbs with the garlic until golden brown and crisp. I like to take them pretty dark, bordering on a little burned, but you do you.
3. Cook the spaghetti in well-salted, boiling water until al dente.
4. Put the mackerel, capers, chile flakes, lemon zest and juice, most of the parsley, and the remaining olive oil into a large mixing bowl and combine thoroughly.
5. Drain the pasta, reserving a little of the water, and add it to the mackerel mixture.
6. Mix vigorously, adding a little pasta water and more olive oil if it seems too dry. You should end up with a glossy sauce that clings to the pasta. Taste and season with salt and black pepper.
7. Serve on a large platter, topped with the pangrattato and the rest of the chopped parsley.

Maple-Glazed Tofu & Garlic Fried Rice

Fried rice is best made with day-old rice, so I tend to make this meal when I have extra rice to use up. Though if you get the craving and you just really want fried rice, you can cook fresh rice and let it cool, then fry—the texture just might be a little more gluey. Tofu gets a bad name for being bland, but I am here to prove to you that, just like a good piece of meat, when handled correctly, it can be heart-stoppingly delicious. This is my favorite way to eat tofu, the texture and the flavor hit all the marks for me. If you want to make this into a more substantial meal, serve with the Sesame Spinach (page 160).

Serves 6–8

For the maple-glazed tofu:

3 (14 oz) packages extra-firm tofu, pressed between sheets of paper towels, to draw out as much moisture as possible

¾ cup cornstarch

½ cup soy sauce (or use tamari to keep this recipe GF)

½ cup maple syrup

½ cup rice vinegar

1 tsp chili oil

a thumb-size piece of ginger, minced

3 garlic cloves, minced

2 cups vegetable oil

For the garlic fried rice:

2 tbsp sesame oil

1 tbsp vegetable oil

3 garlic cloves, minced

3¾ cups cooked white rice, chilled in the fridge, ideally overnight

1 tsp salt

To serve:

toasted sesame seeds

kimchi

chopped green onions

1. Dice the pressed tofu into bite-size chunks and toss in the cornstarch.
2. To make the glaze, mix the soy sauce, maple syrup, rice vinegar, chili oil, ginger, and garlic together in a large saucepan that can hold all the tofu, bring to a boil, then lower to a simmer and allow to thicken and reduce by a third.
3. Heat the vegetable oil in a heavy-bottomed saucepan over medium-high heat. You can check it's the right temperature by dropping in a small piece of bread—if it sinks to the bottom, the oil is still too cold; you want it to float and fry to a golden-brown color.
4. Fry the tofu pieces in batches, until slightly colored and crisp, roughly 2–3 minutes.
5. Drain on paper towels and continue until you have fried all the tofu.
6. Add the tofu to the glaze in the large saucepan and toss until it's all evenly coated. You can keep this over low heat until you are ready to serve.
7. To make the fried rice, heat both oils in a large frying pan—the sesame oil will smoke and smell very fragrant, but don't be alarmed, this is good. Add the garlic and cook until crisp and golden brown, then add the rice and salt. Keep frying until the rice is piping hot and starting to crisp up.
8. Serve the tofu over the rice, with the toasted sesame seeds, kimchi, green onions, and a drizzle more glaze.

A Spring Pea Risotto

Master this base recipe and the risotto world is your oyster. I love risotto with all my heart, but I think it has a reputation for being difficult, long, and laborious. I'm here to convince you otherwise: this is a very simple and classic white risotto that can be on the table in just over an hour, featuring a simple addition of fresh peas. Other great flavor additions and toppings include pesto, confit tomatoes, leftover pasta sauce, and butternut squash purée. We served this risotto at our Spring Supper in 2024 and it was a complete hit.

Serves 6

6⅓ cups vegetable stock
2 tbsp butter of your choice
3 tbsp olive oil, plus extra for drizzling
4 white onions, finely diced
sea salt and black pepper
2½ cups Arborio rice
1 cup dry white wine
juice of 3 lemons
9 oz fresh peas (or frozen, thawed)
3½ oz grated Parmesan, plus extra for topping (omit to keep this recipe vegan)

1. Heat the vegetable stock in a saucepan and keep it simmering gently over low heat so you have it ready to go.
2. Put a large heavy-bottomed pan over medium-high heat and add half the butter and all the olive oil. Once the butter has melted, add the onions, 1 teaspoon of salt, and ½ teaspoon of pepper and sauté until soft and translucent, around 20 minutes.
3. Add the rice and stir to coat with the sticky onions.
4. Add the white wine and lemon juice, stir to deglaze the pan, and allow the rice to absorb all the liquid.
5. Once all the liquid has been absorbed, start adding a few ladles of hot stock at a time, stirring it in and allowing it to absorb before adding the next few ladles. Continue this way until you have used all the stock—this should take about 20 minutes.
6. By now the rice should be cooked and tender. Stir in the peas, all the grated Parmesan, and the remaining tablespoon of butter. Put the lid on the pan and allow it to sit for 5 minutes.
7. Serve the risotto topped with a drizzle of olive oil and a little more grated Parmesan, salt, and pepper.

Baked Beans

Baked beans on toast was a favorite of mine growing up—my dad would make it for lunch, topped with sharp Cheddar cheese and generous black pepper. Canned baked beans hold a special place in my heart, for their cheapness and speed, but this is my version for when you have a little more time on your hands. It is perfect for when you have friends coming round for dinner, and you'd like something delicious yet low effort to feed a crowd. It's affordable, quick, and oh so easy.

Serves 6–8

3 white onions, thinly sliced
4 garlic cloves, thinly sliced
3 tbsp olive oil, plus extra for drizzling
sea salt and black pepper
1 tsp chile flakes
2 tsp dried oregano
2 tsp harissa
1 tsp chipotle paste
2 tbsp tomato paste
1⅔ cups passata (or tomato puree)
1 cup vegetable stock
3 (15 ounce) cans of your favorite beans
2⅔ cups fresh bread crumbs
3½ oz sharp Cheddar, coarsely grated
2 oz Parmesan, finely grated (omit to keep this recipe V)
a few sprigs of thyme, leaves picked

For the salsa:
3 garlic cloves
a small bunch each of chives, mint, and flat-leaf parsley
2 tbsp capers (with 1 tbsp of brine)
½ lemon, quartered, seeds removed
1 tsp Dijon mustard
a pinch each of salt and pepper
7 tbsp extra-virgin olive oil

toasted bread, for serving

1. Preheat the oven to 350°F.
2. In a large saucepan, sauté the onions and garlic in the olive oil, with a pinch of salt and a grind of black pepper, for around 10 minutes, until they are softened and translucent.
3. Add the chile flakes, dried oregano, harissa, chipotle paste, and tomato paste, stir, and keep cooking for another 10 minutes until sticky and starting to color.
4. Add the passata and vegetable stock and bring to a boil, then turn down to a simmer and allow the sauce to reduce for 20 minutes.
5. Rinse the beans, then add to the pan and stir well to combine. Allow to simmer while you make the topping.
6. Make the topping by combining the bread crumbs, Cheddar, Parmesan, a teaspoon each of salt and pepper, and fresh thyme.
7. Pour the bean mix into a large baking dish and top with the cheesy bread crumb mix.
8. Drizzle with a little olive oil and bake in the oven for 30 minutes, until the top is golden brown and the filling is bubbling at the edges.
9. To make the salsa, put all the ingredients into a high-speed blender, including the half lemon, and blend until smooth. Taste and season.
10. Serve the baked beans with a slice of toast and a dollop of the salsa.

Cheese Knödel

Before I had spent any time in Berlin, I had been recommended the same dumpling restaurant numerous times: Knödelwirtschaft. It was almost a year later that I got to try it for myself. After an incessant buildup from friends and people on the internet, these dumplings were at risk of being overhyped. I spent February 2024 in Berlin—it was freezing and dark, the first dinner I ate was knödel, and let me tell you, they lived up to the hype. These are the perfect winter comfort food; they remind me of a combination of Italian malfatti dumplings and the traditional British suet dumplings I had as a child: warming, filling, soft, and plump. I tried lots of interesting flavors of knödel during my time in Berlin, but the cheese dumplings always came out on top—served swimming in butter and laden with Parmesan, with some salad and sauerkraut, they're a real winner.

Makes 12 dumplings

7 slices of soft white bread, diced into small cubes
1 tbsp all-purpose flour
3½ tbsp butter
1 large onion, finely diced
1 garlic clove, minced
3 eggs
⅓ cup milk of your choice
7 oz grated Cheddar cheese
1 tsp sea salt
½ tsp black pepper
1 vegetable bouillon cube

To serve:
7 tbsp butter
2 oz Parmesan (use another hard cheese to keep this recipe V)
a small bunch of chives, finely chopped
sea salt and black pepper
salad and sauerkraut

1. In a large bowl, toss the cubed bread with the flour.
2. Melt the butter in a frying pan, add the onion and garlic, and sauté for 10 minutes until translucent and soft.
3. In a separate bowl, whisk together the eggs and milk.
4. Pour the milk and egg mixture over the bread and add the onion and garlic mix, grated cheese, salt, and pepper. Mix everything by hand, squeezing and kneading until you have a cohesive dumpling dough.
5. Rest the dough in the fridge for 30 minutes.
6. Shape the dough into 12 equal round dumplings, roughly 2 oz each. Or you can use an ice cream scoop, so you get them all an even size. Dipping your hands in water helps stop the dough sticking to them.
7. Bring a large saucepan of water to a boil, add the bouillon cube, and stir until dissolved.
8. Reduce the heat so the water is just under a boil, with no bubbles forming. Add the dumplings and cook for 15 minutes with the lid of the pan ajar—depending on your pan size, you may need to do this in two batches of 6 so that the pan is not too overcrowded. The dumplings should be in one layer.
9. While they cook, melt the butter and grate the Parmesan for serving.

10. Serve the dumplings topped with the melted butter, grated Parmesan, chopped chives, and a pinch each of salt and black pepper. A fresh leafy salad and some sauerkraut also go really well.

Bee's Flammkuchen

I was first introduced to flammkuchen, the traditional German tart, by my brilliant housemate of four years, friend, and photographer for this book—Benedikte Klüver. Bee moved to Berlin in 2023—just before she left we invited friends round to the warehouse to say farewell, and to feed them all we made lots of flammkuchen. She taught me her recipe that evening, and I wrote it down to share with you here. Thank you, Benedikte! The recipe below is our vegetarian version, but you can equally substitute the potato slices with pieces of bacon and omit the sage. This is my favorite thing to eat for dinner when I am in the mood for something exciting, low effort, and high reward.

Makes 1 large flammkuchen

For the dough:
1¾ cups / 240g bread flour, plus extra for dusting
½ cup + 1½ tbsp / 140g water, at room temperature
½ tsp sea salt
2½ tsp olive oil

For the toppings:
⅔ cup / 150ml crème fraîche
1 tsp black pepper
1 tsp sea salt
½ tsp ground nutmeg
1 white onion, very thinly sliced into half-moons
1 medium potato, very thinly sliced into rounds
a handful of sage leaves
olive oil, for drizzling
pinch of flaky sea salt
chili oil, for drizzling (optional)

Equipment:
stand mixer

1. Preheat the oven to 400°F and line your biggest sheet pan with parchment paper.
2. In a stand mixer, with the dough hook attached, combine the flour, water, salt, and olive oil and mix on medium speed until it forms a smooth dough. Knead for 2–3 minutes in the machine at full speed.
3. Turn the dough out onto a floured surface and roll it out into a rectangle the same size as your pan. Transfer the rolled-out dough to the pan. It should be quite thin, and you can stretch it further once on the pan, so that it goes right to the very edges.
4. Mix the crème fraîche with the black pepper, salt, and nutmeg, then spread this mix on top of the dough, going right to the edges.
5. Add the thinly sliced onion in an even layer, followed by the potato slices in a single layer.
6. Toss the sage leaves in a little olive oil and lay them on top of the potatoes.
7. Drizzle the whole flammkuchen with a little more olive oil and add a pinch of flaky salt.
8. Cook on the top rack of the oven for 20 minutes, until the bottom is golden and crisp and the potatoes on top are cooked through.
9. Serve immediately. I like to drizzle a little chili oil on top of mine, but it is not essential.

Sticky Sweet Potatoes, Tahini & Pickled Red Chile

This recipe was born out of a rushed staff lunch with few supplies and a barren walk-in fridge. All I had to play with were sweet potatoes, a few chiles, and the dry store (the pantry of a professional kitchen). What was born out of necessity has become my favorite way to eat sweet potatoes—the warehouse loves them, and I hope you do too. These are great as a side to a chili, another roasted veg, or just eaten on their own with some flatbread to scoop up all the juices.

Serves 6 as a side

For the pickled chiles:
2 medium red chiles, thinly sliced
    into rounds
2 tbsp white wine vinegar
1 tsp sugar
a pinch of sea salt

For the sweet potatoes:
6 large sweet potatoes
1 tbsp olive oil
a pinch of sea salt
2 tbsp maple syrup (or honey)

For the dressing:
6½ tbsp tahini
2 tbsp maple syrup (or honey)
2 tbsp soy sauce (use tamari to keep
    this recipe GF)
juice of 1 lemon

1. Preheat the oven to 400°F and line a sheet pan with parchment paper.
2. Start by pickling the chiles. Mix together all the ingredients in a small bowl, making sure the chiles are submerged in the vinegar and the sugar is dissolved. Set to one side until you are ready to serve.
3. Roughly cut the sweet potatoes—I like mine in rounds roughly ¾ inch thick. Toss with the olive oil and salt and transfer to the lined sheet pan in an even layer. Roast in the oven for 30 minutes, or until cooked through.
4. Add the maple syrup to the potatoes, toss until evenly coated, and return to the oven for another 10 minutes.
5. Make the dressing by whisking all the ingredients together and then thinning out with freshly boiled water. Start with a dash and keep adding until you reach your desired dressing consistency.
6. To assemble, pour half the dressing on a platter, pile the potatoes on top, drizzle with the rest of the dressing, and scatter on the pickled chiles.

Roasted Asparagus, Lemon & Olive Oil

This is my favorite way to eat asparagus, introduced to me by my mum and firmly winning me over to the vegetable as a picky teen eater. You can't go wrong here, it's simple cooking at its best, the perfect addition to any late-spring, early-summer table.

Serves 4 as a side

a bunch of asparagus, woody ends
    trimmed
1 tbsp olive oil
a pinch each of sea salt and black
    pepper
1 lemon

1. Preheat the oven to its highest setting.
2. Place the asparagus on a sheet pan and toss in the olive oil, salt, and pepper.
3. Roast in the oven for 15 minutes, or until crisp and starting to char.
4. Squeeze the juice of the lemon over the asparagus, toss, and serve.
5. These are just as delicious at room temperature as they are hot, so they are a great choice to make in advance.

The Hummus Plate

Hummus is one of the most delicious, healthy, and easy dips in the world—as long as you follow a few simple rules. Use the best-quality chickpeas and tahini you can afford; they are the main ingredients here and will make all the difference. Never add oil as you are blending, as this will cause your hummus to split; instead, use it as a finishing touch once plated. In my opinion, if the tahini and chickpeas are of good-enough quality, it doesn't need any garlic or lemon. The simple recipe below is the one I make time and time again, and it never lets me down.

Serves 6 as a side

2 (15 oz) cans chickpeas, drained and
    rinsed
¼ cup tahini
sea salt
1 tsp ground cumin
black pepper
½ cup ice water
extra-virgin olive oil, for drizzling

Toppings, to elevate:
flat-leaf parsley
diced raw onion
a sprinkle of sumac
a sprinkle of toasted sesame seeds

1. Reserve a scoop of the chickpeas and put them to one side for serving.
2. Place the remaining chickpeas in a food processor or blender with the tahini, ½ teaspoon of salt, cumin, and a good grind of black pepper and blend to a coarse paste.
3. Scrape down the sides and continue to blend, slowly pouring in the ice water with the motor still running, until you have a silky-smooth consistency. You may want to stop and scrape down the sides halfway through to make sure everything is well incorporated and to ensure you don't go past your ideal consistency.
4. Dollop the hummus into the center of a large platter or plate and smooth out the middle to make a well of sorts.
5. Sprinkle over the reserved chickpeas and drizzle with good-quality extra-virgin olive oil, a pinch of salt, and a grind of black pepper, along with any of the other toppings.

Jammy Shallot Harissa Bulgur

This is a simple and delicious way to cook bulgur wheat with a little more flavor and texture than serving it plain. It's great alongside other mezze dishes, as the base of a salad, or a perfect sharing picnic addition. This dish is lovely eaten hot but even better at room temperature, making it a good one to do in advance if you are short on time. Make a batch of this to keep in your fridge and elevate meals all week long—it's the more exciting cousin to adding a piece of bread to your lunch!

Serves 6 as a side

4 large banana shallots, thinly sliced
2 tbsp olive oil, plus extra for drizzling
a pinch each of sea salt and black
    pepper
1 tsp ground cinnamon
1 tsp ground cumin
1 tbsp tomato paste
1 tbsp harissa
1⅔ cups vegetable stock
1 tsp red wine vinegar, plus extra for
    topping
1¾ cups bulgur wheat
a small bunch of soft herbs such as
    flat-leaf parsley, dill, or cilantro,
    roughly chopped

1. In a medium saucepan with a tight-fitting lid, sauté the shallots with the olive oil, salt, and pepper over medium-high heat for up to 20 minutes, until they are jammy and caramelized.
2. Add the ground cinnamon, cumin, tomato paste, and harissa. Stir to combine and keep cooking for another 2–3 minutes.
3. Add the vegetable stock and red wine vinegar and bring to a boil for 5 minutes.
4. Add the bulgur wheat, stir until well distributed, then put the lid on the pan and turn the heat off, leaving the bulgur to absorb all the liquid for 30 minutes.
5. Remove the lid and fluff up the bulgur until no clumps remain, then turn out onto a platter and top with the soft herbs, a drizzle of olive oil, and a splash more red wine vinegar.

Harissa Honey Roasted Carrots, Tahini Yogurt & Sesame Seeds

These carrots hit all the right notes for me, their natural sweetness enhanced by the honey, complemented by the heat of the harissa, contrasting with the sharpness of the yogurt, and held together by the creamy nuttiness of the sesame. It's a flavor, texture, and color hit; the leftovers make a very good sandwich filling with a little crunchy lettuce. This dish is great served alongside flatbreads, dips, and salads as a mezze, or simply on its own with some good bread to scoop everything up.

Serves 4 as a main or 8 as a side

6½ tbsp harissa

2 garlic cloves, minced

1 tbsp honey (or maple syrup),
    plus extra for drizzling

1 tbsp olive oil

1 tsp ground cumin

1 tsp sea salt

½ tsp black pepper

2¼ lb carrots, trimmed and
    scrubbed clean

1¼ cups yogurt of your choice

2 tbsp tahini

zest of 1 lemon

2 tbsp sesame seeds

flaky sea salt

1. Preheat the oven to 350°F.
2. In a bowl, whisk together the harissa, garlic, honey, olive oil, ground cumin, sea salt, and pepper.
3. Toss the carrots in the harissa mix in a large sheet pan—there's no need to peel or chop them, just make sure they are clean and of a similar thickness, halving any huge ones if necessary.
4. Roast in the oven for 1 hour 20 minutes, or until a knife easily passes through the middle of the thickest carrot, basting with the glaze halfway through.
5. Set the carrots to one side until you are ready to serve.
6. Whisk together the yogurt, tahini, and lemon zest, spread this in thick swoops on a large platter, pile the carrots on top, and sprinkle with the sesame seeds.
7. Drizzle with a little more honey and sprinkle some flaky salt over the top just before serving.

Hasselback Potatoes, Miso Almond Sauce, Massaged Kale & Lemon Dressing

This is a recipe I developed in the dead of winter, too far away from the spring produce coming into season and in a bit of a rut with the winter vegetables. I wanted something bright and zingy, and all I had to work with was potatoes and kale. Then a massive delivery of citrus arrived at work, direct from Sicily, and I was inspired, and encouraged, to use up a lot of lemons—hence this salad was born. It's citrusy and light, yet nourishing. There's some exciting textures and a deeply comforting umami vibe from the miso almond sauce.

Serves 4–6 as a main, 6–8 as a side

For the potatoes and kale:
1½ lb new potatoes
3 tbsp olive oil
2 tsp sea salt
½ tsp black pepper
4½ oz kale

For the miso almond dressing:
1¾ cups almond flour
1 tbsp brown rice miso
4 tsp sherry vinegar
2 tbsp + 2 tsp olive oil

For the salsa:
2 lemons
½ red onion, finely diced
a small bunch of flat-leaf parsley,
   finely chopped
1 tsp chile flakes
1 tbsp olive oil
sea salt and black pepper

To serve:
3½ oz toasted sliced almonds

1. Preheat the oven to 350°F.
2. Hasselback the potatoes: for ease and speed, slice the potato in the dip of a wooden spoon—the edges of the spoon stop the knife from going all the way through. Place the potatoes in a large roasting pan and toss with 2 tablespoons of the olive oil, 1 teaspoon of the salt, and the pepper. Roast for 1 hour, or until golden brown, crisp, and cooked through.
3. Pour boiling water over the almond flour in a small bowl, enough to cover. Stir, then set aside to soak.
4. Wash the kale and mix with the remaining tablespoon of olive oil and remaining teaspoon of salt. Really massage the oil and salt into the kale with your hands—this breaks down the fibers and makes it easier to digest.
5. Drain the almond flour, reserving a few tablespoons of the milky soaking water. Blend the almond flour with the miso, vinegar, and olive oil, thinning it out with the almond water until it reaches Greek yogurt consistency.
6. To make the salsa, with a sharp knife cut away all the peel and pith from the lemons, revealing the flesh of the fruit. Finely dice the flesh, removing any seeds.
7. Mix the diced lemon with the red onion, parsley, chile flakes, olive oil, and a pinch of salt and pepper.
8. To assemble, take a large platter, add all the miso almond dressing, lay half the kale on top, then half the potatoes, then repeat. Scatter the salsa on top and finish by sprinkling with the sliced almonds.

Sesame Spinach

This is my favorite way to eat spinach, without a doubt, and I crave it all year round. If you can't find Chinese sesame paste, tahini will work fine, but if you do have a good Asian supermarket nearby, I encourage you to go there! They have the best selections of chili oils (Lao Gan Ma for life), kimchi, and bulk spices—and this sesame paste alone is worth the trip. Trust me on the spinach quantities; you need a lot, as it wilts down to nothing, and once you have tried it with the sauce you will be wishing you'd made more. This is perfect to serve as a side over rice, or it goes very well with the Maple-Glazed Tofu on page 140.

Serves 6 as a side

2¼ lb loose leaf spinach

For the sesame sauce:
3 tbsp Chinese sesame paste (or tahini)
3 tbsp soy sauce*
3 tbsp dark soy sauce*
1 tsp rice vinegar
1 tsp sesame oil
1 tsp sugar
1 tsp chili oil
1 tsp cold water

To serve:
a handful of toasted sesame seeds

* substitute with tamari to keep this recipe GF

1. Wilt the spinach in salted boiling water, then drain, and once cool enough to handle, squeeze out as much liquid as possible. Roughly chop and set aside.
2. To make the sauce, whisk together all the ingredients until smooth.
3. Pour the sesame sauce into a dish, pile the spinach on top, and sprinkle with the toasted sesame seeds to finish.

Last of the Summer Tomatoes, Roasted Squash & Brown Butter Hazelnuts

This was the starter at our first Fall Supper Club at the beginning of October 2023, just as the very last of the summer tomatoes were coming in from the Isle of Wight. Paired with the iconically autumnal nutty squash, it felt like a beautiful way to say goodbye to summer and welcome the cooler months, while being completely delicious too. So many of our supper club guests asked what I had done to the vegetables to make them taste so good, and the answer really was not much—if you cook with seasonal, local ingredients, you will find they do all the hard work for you. If you don't have time to slow-cook the tomatoes, they will be fine cooked for the same time and temperature as the squash, although they may not hold their shape as well.

Serves 6

6–10 ripe plum, beefsteak, or vine tomatoes, halved

2 tbsp olive oil, plus extra for drizzling sea salt

1 large squash (butternut or acorn)

½ tsp black pepper

7 tbsp unsalted butter of your choice

½ cup roasted peeled hazelnuts, finely chopped

1. Preheat the oven to 300°F. Line a large sheet pan with parchment paper.
2. Place the tomatoes in a single layer, cut side up, on the pan and drizzle with a tiny bit of olive oil and a pinch of sea salt.
3. Slow-cook in the oven for 2 hours—this will dehydrate them slightly and develop the natural sugars, resulting in a sweet semi-dried tomato that still bears some juicy goodness.
4. Once the tomatoes are out of the oven, turn the heat up to 400°F.
5. Halve and seed the squash, then, leaving the skin on, cut into half-moons about 1½ inches thick.
6. In a large bowl, toss the squash with the olive oil, 1 teaspoon of salt, and the pepper. Lay all the squash on another sheet pan and cook in the oven for 1 hour 20 minutes, flipping the pieces halfway through so they color evenly. You are looking for a crisp golden-brown exterior and a soft, squishy interior—this may take more or less time depending on your oven, so check after 40 minutes and see how they are doing.
7. Meanwhile, melt the butter in a small saucepan and keep cooking, swirling the melted butter until the milk solids have turned a nutty brown.

8. Take the pan off the heat and add the hazelnuts to the browned butter with a pinch of salt. It will foam up, but keep stirring for a few minutes, then set to one side.

9. When you are ready to serve, take a large platter and layer the squash with the tomatoes. Scatter on the hazelnuts and drizzle the browned butter over the top.

Minted Garden Peas, Fava Beans & Sizzled Green Onions over Whipped Lemony Ricotta

This is perfect as a light summer dinner, served with fresh bread, or as a side to a bigger meal. I love the sweetness of fresh garden peas against the creamy ricotta, balanced out with lots of acidic lemon juice and zest. This salad comes together in a flash and is a great one to do ahead, as you can prepare all the elements up to 3 days in advance and then assemble just before eating.

Serves 4 as a main or 6 as a side

1 (15 oz) container ricotta
4 lemons
3 tbsp olive oil, plus extra for drizzling
sea salt and black pepper
14 oz (about 2⅔ cups) garden peas
   (fresh are best, frozen will do)
9 oz (about 1¾ cups) shelled fava
   beans (fresh are best, frozen will do)
a large bunch of mint
a large bunch of green onions,
   trimmed and cleaned
bread of your choice, for serving

1. In a food processor, or in a large mixing bowl by hand, whip the ricotta, the zest and juice of 1 lemon, 1 tablespoon of the olive oil, a pinch of salt, and a grind of black pepper until smooth. The mix should be silky and smooth but still hold its shape. Taste and adjust the seasoning with more salt, black pepper, or lemon juice, to suit your palate. I like mine heavy on the lemon and black pepper.
2. Cook the peas and fava beans in salted boiling water until tender, around 2 minutes, then refresh in ice water.
3. Drain the peas and beans and put them into a large bowl.
4. Roughly chop the mint and add it to the bowl with the zest and juice of 2 lemons, the remaining olive oil, and a good pinch of salt and pepper. Mix and set to one side.
5. In a grill pan over medium-high heat, cook the green onions with a little olive oil, salt, and pepper until softened and charred. Halve the final lemon and add the halves to the pan cut side down, allowing the inside of the lemon to become charred as well.
6. To assemble, dollop the ricotta onto a large platter and spread it out into glamorous swoops.
7. Pile the pea, fava bean, and mint mixture on top, add the charred green onions, and finally squeeze over all the juice from the charred lemons.
8. Drizzle with more olive oil, sprinkle with salt and pepper, and serve immediately with a hunk of bread.

A Summer Feast

In the summer, I like to cook lots of delicious things in big batches, to share over dinner with friends, or to keep my fridge stocked all week with perfect bites. These dishes go well together in a meal but also are great on their own; they last well in the fridge, some might even say they get better, and they showcase the very best of summer produce. If you can, eat them outdoors, with the sun on your face—it's scientifically proven to taste better.

Serves 6–8

For the marinated vegetables:

3 medium eggplants, sliced into rounds

3 medium zucchini, sliced into rounds

1 tbsp sea salt

6 tbsp extra-virgin olive oil

2 tbsp red wine vinegar

3 garlic cloves, minced

½ tsp dried oregano

For the herbed bulgur:

2 cups bulgur wheat

1 vegetable bouillon cube

1 tbsp olive oil

1 tsp sea salt

½ tsp black pepper

a bunch of flat-leaf parsley, finely chopped

a bunch of dill, finely chopped

a bunch of chives, finely chopped

zest and juice of 1 lemon

To make the marinated vegetables:

1. Preheat the broiler to its highest setting, or heat a heavy cast-iron grill pan over high heat.
2. Toss the eggplant and zucchini slices in a large colander with the salt. Set the colander to one side for 20 minutes in the sink while the vegetables release their water.
3. Pat the vegetables dry, then lay them in a single layer either on a baking sheet under the broiler or in the grill pan. Broil or pan-grill until one side has turned golden brown, then turn and repeat on the other side. A little bit of char here is nice, so don't worry if parts are blackened.
4. Repeat with all the eggplant and zucchini slices.
5. Combine the grilled vegetables in a big bowl with the olive oil, red wine vinegar, garlic, and oregano, mix well to combine, and set aside to marinate at room temperature until you are ready to serve.

To make the herbed bulgur:

1. Rinse the bulgur thoroughly under running water, then place in a large bowl.
2. Crumble in the bouillon cube, cover with freshly boiled water, and stir to combine.
3. Cover the bowl and set to one side for 30 minutes to allow the bulgur to absorb all the stock.
4. When you are ready to serve, fluff up the grains with a fork and stir in the olive oil, salt, pepper, chopped herbs, and lemon zest and juice.

For the tomatoes:

2¼ lb of the most ripe, juicy, sweet
    tomatoes you can find

1 tsp sea salt

2 tbsp extra-virgin olive oil

For the walnuts:

1 cup walnuts

1 tsp olive oil

1 tsp sea salt

For the tahini dressing:

⅔ cup tahini

1 garlic clove, minced

juice of ½ lemon

1 tsp sea salt

½ tsp black pepper

For serving:

hot sauce (optional)

chili oil (optional)

For the tomatoes:

1. Simply slice, sprinkle with the salt, and drizzle with the
   olive oil.

For the walnuts:

1. Preheat the oven to 400°F.

2. Roast the walnuts on a baking sheet for 8–10 minutes,
   until just starting to brown.

3. Take out of the oven and toss with the olive oil and salt.
   Allow to cool to room temperature before serving.

For the tahini dressing:

1. Whisk together all the ingredients into a smooth paste,
   then thin out with enough ice water to reach the
   consistency of plain yogurt.

To serve:

1. Pile your plates high with the herbed bulgur, marinated
   vegetables, salted tomatoes, roasted walnuts, and drizzle
   with tahini dressing. A splash of good hot sauce doesn't
   go amiss here either, and chili oil would be a welcome
   addition in the warehouse.

Black Bean Chili & Charred Corn Salsa

There is nothing like a big pot of chili on a cold winter's evening to warm your bones and your soul. This version has a delicious depth of flavor from the coffee, cocoa powder, and dried chiles. Try to get your hands on dried chipotles if you can, they provide the perfect smoky-sweet flavor without being overpoweringly hot.

Serves 6–8

2 dried chipotle or ancho chiles
7 tbsp strong hot black coffee
2 tbsp vegetable oil
2 white onions, diced
3 garlic cloves, crushed
2 tsp sea salt
2 tsp ground cumin
4 tsp smoked paprika
2 tsp cocoa powder
2 tbsp tomato paste
2 (15 oz) cans black beans
2 (15 oz) cans red kidney beans
1⅔ cups vegetable stock
1 tbsp cider vinegar
1 tbsp brown sugar
2 (14.5 oz) cans crushed tomatoes

For the salsa:
1 (11 oz) can corn kernels
1 medium red onion, finely diced
1 medium plum tomato, finely diced
a small bunch of cilantro, finely chopped
juice of 2 limes
1 tbsp olive oil
sea salt and black pepper

To serve:
steamed rice
sour cream
grated Cheddar cheese
tortilla chips

1. Put the dried chiles into a small bowl and pour in the hot coffee. Cover and set to one side to rehydrate.
2. In a large heavy-bottomed pan, heat the vegetable oil and add the onions, garlic, and salt. Cook for 10 minutes, until softened and turning translucent.
3. Add the cumin, paprika, and cocoa powder and continue to cook, stirring occasionally, for 2–3 minutes.
4. Add the tomato paste and stir to combine.
5. Blend the chiles and coffee with an immersion blender or in a blender until smooth, then add this to the pan and stir to combine.
6. Add the beans (including their liquid), stock, vinegar, brown sugar, and canned tomatoes.
7. Stir to combine, bring to a boil, then reduce to a simmer for at least 1 hour, or as long as 3 hours, stirring occasionally. The longer you simmer, the better it will taste.
8. To make the salsa, heat a large frying pan over medium-high heat until very hot. Drain the corn, add to the pan, and leave to char, tossing occasionally to get an even color. The corn should be almost blackened in places, charred, smoky, and have a chewy dried-out texture.
9. Toss the charred corn with the onion, tomato, cilantro, lime juice, olive oil, and season to taste with salt and pepper.
10. Serve the chili over rice with a dollop of sour cream, a handful of grated sharp Cheddar, and a good helping of salsa. Tortilla chips are also a must.

Cacio e Pepe

This is my favorite of the four classic Roman pastas (cacio e pepe, carbonara, Amatriciana, alla Gricia). The name simply means "cheese and pepper." It only has three ingredients and encompasses the true essence of Italian cuisine: simple, good-quality ingredients, cooked with care. If you can, I would encourage you to ask for help when mixing in the sauce; it helps to have a second pair of hands to pour while you hold the pan and mix vigorously. The key to getting the sauce just right is to mix and add the cheese over low heat until you reach emulsification, which is tricky to do on your own. Once the pasta is cooked, things move quickly, so make sure you have all your ingredients ready to go before you start cooking the pasta—mise en place!

Serves 6

1 lb 5 oz bucatini (or spaghetti)
1 lb Pecorino Romano, finely grated (it's very important to use Pecorino Romano here, rather than the young soft pecorino), plus extra for topping
4 tsp freshly ground black pepper (you're going to think this is a lot, but go with it), plus extra as needed
sea salt

1. Cook the pasta until al dente, in heavily salted water.
2. Put three-quarters of the grated pecorino into a large bowl. Reserve the rest for topping or adding to the sauce later.
3. While the pasta is cooking, add a small ladle of pasta water to the big bowl of cheese and whisk until a thick, creamy sauce forms.
4. Toast the ground black pepper in a large dry frying pan over medium heat, until fragrant, 2–3 minutes.
5. Add a small ladle of pasta water to the black pepper pan and lower the heat to the lowest setting.
6. Once the pasta is cooked, reserve a cup of the pasta water, then drain the pasta, add to the black pepper pan, and toss until well combined.
7. Next, slowly pour the cheese mixture into the pasta, tossing and mixing all the time.
8. Keep mixing vigorously, adding a little more pasta water or pecorino to reach your desired consistency. You are looking for a smooth, creamy, emulsified sauce that coats the pasta. If it looks dry, add more pasta water, and if it looks watery, add more cheese from the reserved quarter.
9. Serve immediately, and if you are like me, top with more cheese, salt, and black pepper!

Caponata, Fried Bread & Couscous

This is one of my favorite things to eat in summer as a light lunch or supper. It's just the perfect hot-weather meal, and no surprise, as its roots are in Sicily and the Middle East. This is one of those dishes that gets better with time, as the flavors get to know each other, so make a big batch and see how long you can drag it out for. I ate some wonderful versions on a vacation in Sicily, each slightly different from the last, and this is my ode to the beautiful Mediterranean island.

Serves 6

2 eggplants, diced
2 zucchini, diced
1 tbsp table salt
2 cups vegetable oil, for deep-frying
2 tbsp olive oil
2 white onions, finely diced
4 stalks of celery, finely diced
1 tsp chile flakes
sea salt
2 tbsp tomato paste
6 fresh plum tomatoes, diced
6 tbsp capers
3 oz (⅔ cup) pitted Kalamata olives
¾ cup golden raisins
1 tbsp white wine vinegar, plus extra as needed
1 tbsp sugar, plus extra as needed
1 (14.5 oz) can chopped tomatoes

To serve:
1 lb couscous
1 cup sliced almonds
a small bunch of flat-leaf parsley
6 slices of crusty bread
olive oil, for frying

1. In a large colander, toss the diced eggplants and zucchini in the table salt, then set the colander over a bowl or in the sink to catch the liquid. Let drain for 30 minutes.
2. Heat the vegetable oil in a saucepan over medium-high heat and fry the eggplants and zucchini in batches, until golden brown, then drain on paper towels and set to one side.
3. Heat the olive oil in a large heavy-bottomed pan and sauté the onions, celery, chile flakes, and ½ teaspoon of salt for 10 minutes, until softened and translucent.
4. Add the tomato paste, stir to combine, and cook for 5 minutes longer. Add the fresh tomatoes and cook for another 10 minutes, until broken down and saucy.
5. Add the capers, olives, raisins, vinegar, sugar, and canned tomatoes and bring to a boil.
6. Add the fried eggplants and zucchini, then turn down the heat and let simmer for 20 minutes.
7. Turn off the heat and allow to cool in the pan to room temperature. Taste for seasoning and add more salt, sugar, or vinegar as necessary.
8. When you are ready to serve, cook the couscous, toast the sliced almonds, roughly chop the parsley, and fry the slices of bread in a little olive oil until golden brown on both sides.
9. Serve the caponata over couscous, sprinkled with the parsley and sliced almonds, with a slice of fried bread.

Gnocchi alla Sorrentina

This is a dish that Virginia introduced to me, and my life has never been the same since. I love making fresh gnocchi and eating it simply, but there is something oh so luxurious and comforting about this baked version. It utilizes premade store-bought gnocchi, so it's an incredibly simple and easy recipe with a high reward. Make it on one of those cold, dark, rainy winter days and have your world turned upside down.

Serves 6–8

2 tbsp olive oil, plus extra for drizzling
8 garlic cloves, crushed
a large bunch of basil, stems finely chopped, leaves separated
sea salt and black pepper
1 tbsp tomato paste
3 (14.5 oz) cans chopped tomatoes (I use Polpa; whole peeled are also a great option, crushed by hand before adding to the pot)
1 tsp red wine vinegar
2¼ lb store-bought potato gnocchi
3 (8 oz) balls of mozzarella, roughly diced into cubes
grated Parmesan, for topping (use another hard cheese to keep this recipe V)

1. Preheat the oven to 425°F.
2. Heat a large pan over medium-high heat, add the olive oil and the crushed garlic, cook for a few minutes and then add the basil stems. Season with a pinch of salt and a grind of black pepper and keep cooking for 2–3 minutes.
3. Add the tomato paste, stir to combine, cook for another 3 minutes, then add the canned tomatoes and red wine vinegar. Bring to a boil, then lower the heat and simmer for 20 minutes.
4. Meanwhile, bring a large saucepan of salted water to a boil.
5. Add the gnocchi and cook for 2–3 minutes, until each piece floats to the top of the pan. You may want to do this in two batches, depending on the size of your pan.
6. Add the basil leaves and half the mozzarella to the tomato sauce and stir until it's all melted in.
7. Add the cooked gnocchi to the tomato mozzarella sauce, stir to combine, and then pour the whole mix into an oiled ovenproof dish.
8. Top with the rest of the mozzarella and add a good grating of Parmesan, a drizzle of olive oil, and a pinch of salt and pepper.
9. Bake in the oven for 30 minutes, until the top is crisp and the sauce is bubbling up at the sides.

Macaroni Cheese

My dad taught me how to make a béchamel sauce when I was ten or eleven years old, and it was both fascinating and thrilling. I always think of him when I make one now. We didn't measure anything, instead working by eye and the size of the pan; béchamel is a great way to hone your instincts, it's about watching, waiting, and feeling. Growing up, macaroni cheese was firmly a winter food, and I have strong memories of trudging home from school in the snow, toes numb from the cold, and finding my mum at the stove, stirring a big pot of it. It was the best feeling. I was so obsessed that I would sneak downstairs and eat the leftovers cold. My secret to balancing the sauce is to use plant-based milk, which reaps a lighter, less overwhelming sauce that leaves more room for seconds. Any cheese works well, but I like to have a sharp Cheddar base and add from there.

Serves 6–8

2¼ lb rigatoni (or macaroni)

½ cup + 1 tbsp unsalted butter, plus extra for greasing the dish

1 cup all-purpose flour

5½ cups plant-based milk (I use oat)

1½ lb hard cheese, such as mature Cheddar, Comté, red Leicester, or a mix of all three, grated

sea salt and black pepper

2 tbsp Dijon mustard

2 oz Parmesan, grated (use another hard cheese to keep this recipe V)

olive oil, for drizzling

hot sauce, for serving (optional)

1. Preheat the oven 400°F.
2. Cook the pasta in heavily salted water for 5 minutes less than the cooking time given on the package—we want it under al dente as it will continue cooking in the oven. Drain and set to one side.
3. To make the sauce, melt the butter in a large heavy-bottomed pan, and once it is completely melted, whisk in the flour to make a paste or a roux. Cook the roux for 2 minutes, stirring all the time.
4. Slowly whisk in the milk until it is all incorporated and there are no lumps of flour. Keep whisking over medium heat until the sauce has thickened, making sure it doesn't catch on the bottom.
5. Once the sauce has thickened, whisk in the grated cheese until melted, then add 2 teaspoons each of salt and pepper, and Dijon mustard. Taste and adjust the seasoning as necessary.
6. Combine the cooked pasta and sauce in a large, buttered ovenproof dish. Top with the grated Parmesan, a drizzle of olive oil, and a little more salt and pepper.
7. Bake for 30 minutes, or until the top is golden brown and crisp and the sauce is bubbling up around the edges.
8. Let stand for 10 minutes before serving. I eat mine with a good few dashes of a sharp hot sauce, such as Tabasco.

Potato & Pineapple Massaman Curry

I know this sounds strange, but hear me out. When I first moved to London, I spent a brief period working at an events company, and the highlight of the working week was on Thursdays, when we would head down to Whitecross Market, in Farringdon, for our lunch. There was a food truck that sold "buddha bowls": perfectly cooked short-grain brown rice under a potato and pineapple Massaman curry. I was not sold on the pineapple thing, but after one bowl I was hooked, and I have been trying to re-create their version ever since. Even if you think you don't like pineapple in savory food, be brave, trust me, and make this curry.

Serves 6–8

2 tbsp vegetable oil, plus a little for the tofu
6 banana shallots, thinly sliced
a pinch of sea salt
⅔ cup Massaman paste
1 lb baby potatoes, halved
1 tsp ground cinnamon
2 tbsp soy sauce (or use tamari to keep this recipe GF)
2 tbsp dark brown sugar
½ cup + 1½ tbsp creamy peanut butter
2 (13.5 oz) cans full-fat coconut milk
7 oz smoked tofu, cubed
1 (15.5 oz) can pineapple chunks
7 oz green beans, trimmed and halved
juice of 2 limes

To serve:
steamed rice
salted peanuts, roughly chopped
cilantro leaves
sriracha

1. Put the vegetable oil, shallots, and salt into a large heavy-bottomed pan, over medium heat. Cook for 15 minutes, stirring occasionally, until the shallots are starting to take on some color.
2. Add the Massaman paste and cook for another 5 minutes.
3. Add the potatoes, cinnamon, soy sauce, brown sugar, peanut butter, and coconut milk. Fill one of the empty coconut milk cans with boiling water and add that too. Stir everything together, turn up the heat, and bring the sauce to a boil. Reduce to a simmer and cook until the potatoes are cooked through, around 40 minutes, depending on the size of your potatoes.
4. Keep an eye on the pot and stir occasionally to stop the bottom from catching.
5. In a separate pan, over medium-high heat, fry the cubed tofu in a little vegetable oil, until the sides are brown and crisp.
6. When the potatoes are cooked, add the fried tofu, pineapple, green beans, and lime juice and cook for another 5 minutes. I like the beans to have a crunch to them, but cook a little longer if you prefer them soft.
7. Serve the curry over steamed rice, topped with salted peanuts, some cilantro leaves, and a healthy drizzle of sriracha.

Roasted Squash, Browned Butter, Crispy Sage, Hazelnuts & Wilted Lacinato Kale

This recipe screams autumn, and it's inspired by my favorite stuffed pasta, tortelli di zucca burro e salvia. But there are very few days of the year when I have the time to make stuffed pasta, and when I crave these flavors, I make this salad. You can of course cook some pasta—orzo would be good here—and toss that in as well, to make a more filling meal.

Serves 6

2¼ lb winter squash
2 tbsp olive oil, plus extra for drizzling
sea salt and black pepper
7 oz lacinato kale, stripped from the stem and roughly chopped
7 tbsp butter
1 cup hazelnuts
a handful of sage leaves
shaved Parmesan, for topping (use another hard cheese to keep this recipe V)

1. Preheat the oven to 350°F.
2. Halve and seed the squash, then slice into half-moons, leaving the skin on.
3. In a large roasting pan, toss the squash with the olive oil, 2 teaspoons of salt, and 1 teaspoon of pepper.
4. Roast the squash for 40 minutes, then flip each piece and roast for 20 minutes longer, until crisp and golden on the outside but soft within.
5. Blanch the kale in well-salted water, then drain and drizzle in a little olive oil and season with salt and pepper.
6. Melt the butter in a saucepan over medium-high heat; once it starts to bubble, add the hazelnuts and the sage leaves, stirring until they are nicely browned and the leaves are crisp. Take the pan off the heat and set to one side.
7. Layer the kale and roasted squash over a large serving platter. Drizzle with the butter and scatter the hazelnuts and sage on top.
8. Top with shaved Parmesan and a final twist of black pepper.

Sri Lankan Dal with Coconut Sambal

This is my version of the delicious dal and sambal I ate every day on Hiriketiya Beach in Sri Lanka when I visited back in 2019. It's as close as I have got to re-creating it at home. This is an incredibly easy recipe, healthy, affordable, just so happens to be vegan, and is one of my go-to dinners in the colder months. The sambal is the real star of the show and brings the bowl together—it's sharp, salty, and sweet, and packs a punch with the heat from the chile. Traditionally you would use fresh coconut in the sambal—here I have used shredded dried and rehydrated it in boiling water to mimic the texture of fresh. Serve with rice or Bee's Potato Flatbreads (page 98) and you have a hearty, healthy, delicious meal on the table in under an hour.

Serves 6–8

For the dal:
2 cups red lentils
1 tsp ground turmeric
1 tsp sea salt
2 (13.5 oz) cans coconut milk

For the temper:
2 tbsp vegetable oil
6 garlic cloves, thinly sliced
2 white onions, roughly chopped
7 oz (about 1½ cups) cherry tomatoes, halved
1 tsp sea salt
2 tsp ground cumin
2 tsp coriander seeds
2 tsp black mustard seeds

For the sambal:
9 oz shredded dried coconut
2 large red chiles, stems removed
juice of 2 limes, plus extra as needed
sea salt
2 tbsp sugar, plus extra as needed
3 shallots, finely diced

1. To make the dal, thoroughly wash the lentils, then place them in a big saucepan with the turmeric and salt. Cover with cold water and bring to a boil over medium-high heat. Lower the heat and simmer, stirring occasionally, until all the water has been absorbed.
2. Meanwhile, heat the coconut milk in a separate pan. Once the dal has absorbed all the water, add the coconut milk and stir to combine. Keep the dal simmering away over low heat.
3. To make the temper, heat the vegetable oil in a frying pan and add the garlic, onion, tomatoes, salt, and spices. Cook for around 20 minutes, until the veg have cooked down, started to color, and are smelling fragrant. Add this mix to the dal and stir well to combine. Keep the dal simmering over low heat while you make the sambal.
4. Meanwhile, make the sambal. Put the shredded coconut into a bowl, cover with boiling water, and let soak for 10 minutes.
5. Using a mortar and pestle, or a blender, combine the red chiles, lime juice, 2 teaspoons of salt, and the sugar until a bright red paste forms.
6. Drain the coconut, getting out as much water as possible, and mix with the chile-lime paste and the shallots until the coconut takes on a red hue. Taste and adjust the seasoning with more lime, sugar, or salt depending on your preference.

To serve:
rice (or potato flatbreads)
fresh cilantro leaves
lime wedges
chili oil (optional)

7. Serve generous bowls of dal over rice or potato flatbreads, topped with the sambal, fresh cilantro leaves, wedges of lime, and chili oil if you want to kick up the heat.

Mezze Feast

There are a few recipes here that I suggest making together to reap an abundant mezze feast. If you do it as written, this is an afternoon's work that's best saved for a rainy day. However, you can of course make them independently of each other, and they will be just as good. The hot sauce makes enough for a couple of meals and will keep well in your fridge for up to a week.

Serves 6–8

For the falafel:
2 cups dried chickpeas (soaked overnight in lots of cold water, making sure the container leaves enough room for them to triple in size)
½ medium white onion
3 garlic cloves
a small bunch each of fresh flat-leaf parsley, cilantro, and dill
2 tsp ground coriander
1 tbsp ground cumin
1 tsp baking powder
1 tbsp all-purpose flour
2 tsp salt
¾ cup sesame seeds
4 cups sunflower oil, for frying

For the garlic tahini sauce:
1 cup tahini
2 garlic cloves, minced
juice of 1 lemon
sea salt and black pepper

To make the falafel:
1. Drain the soaked chickpeas and put them into a large bowl with all the falafel ingredients except the sesame seeds and sunflower oil. Give everything a good mix.
2. Working in batches, blend the falafel mix in a food processor until it's fine and almost a paste consistency. Chill the mix in the fridge for 30 minutes.
3. The mix should hold when you squeeze it in your hand. Roll it into balls that are roughly the size of a golf ball and weigh about 1½ oz each. You should get roughly 24 balls of falafel.
4. Roll the falafel in the sesame seeds. Heat the sunflower oil in a large saucepan and deep-fry the falafel in batches over medium-high heat. To check that the oil is at the right temperature, add a small amount of the falafel mixture. If it sinks to the bottom the oil is too cold, if it floats and bubbles away then it's hot enough. Fry the falafel for 4–5 minutes. If the oil is too hot, the outside will brown too much before the inside is cooked, so test one falafel before going to town on the rest.

To make the garlic tahini sauce:
1. Put the tahini, garlic, and lemon juice into a small bowl and whisk to combine.
2. Whisk in enough ice water to reach your desired consistency, season with salt and pepper, and serve.

For the flatbreads:

1 tsp sugar

2 tsp salt

1 tbsp instant yeast

1 cup + 1 tbsp warm water

2⅔ cups bread flour, plus extra
for dusting

For the sumac onion slaw:

1 head of green cabbage

1 white onion

a small bunch of dill, finely chopped

1 tbsp white wine vinegar

2 tbsp olive oil

2 tsp sea salt

1 tsp black pepper

1 tbsp sumac

For the hot sauce:

1 tsp + 1 tbsp olive oil

6 red chiles (as hot as you dare),
roughly chopped

1 white onion, roughly chopped

4 garlic cloves, roughly chopped

12 oz (drained weight) jarred roasted
red peppers, roughly chopped

1 tsp each of sea salt and black pepper

2 tbsp white wine vinegar

Equipment:

stand mixer

To make the flatbreads:

1. In the bowl of a stand mixer, combine the sugar, salt, yeast, and warm water. Mix to combine, then let sit for the yeast to bloom for 5 minutes and become lively and bubbly.

2. Add the flour to the bowl, and with the dough hook fitted, mix on medium speed for 5 minutes, until a smooth elastic dough forms.

3. Put the dough into a lightly oiled bowl and cover with a kitchen towel. Set aside somewhere warm and allow to rise for 1 hour, or until doubled in size (see Top Tip).

4. Split the dough equally into 8 pieces, shape into tight balls, and leave, loosely covered, to proof again for 30 minutes.

5. When you are ready to cook the flatbreads, take a rolling pin and roll them out on a well-floured surface, to about the thickness of a quarter.

6. Cook them one at a time in a roaring-hot dry frying pan, flipping once to ensure both sides cook through. The flatbread should puff up like a balloon—this is great and fun.

7. Wrap the cooked flatbreads in a clean kitchen towel to keep warm while you cook the rest. Serve immediately.

Top Tip: Make the dough to step 3 and rather than leaving it somewhere warm to rise for an hour, pop the dough in the fridge overnight and pick up the method at step 4 the following day, a few hours before serving.

To make the sumac onion slaw:

1. Shred the cabbage and the onion, either on a mandoline or with a sharp knife.

2. In a large bowl, mix all the ingredients with your hands, really scrunching up the cabbage and massaging the dressing in. Serve immediately.

To make the hot sauce:

1. In a small saucepan, over medium-high heat, heat 1 teaspoon of olive oil and add the chiles, onion, garlic, roasted red peppers, salt, and pepper. Cook for 5–10 minutes, until everything has softened.

2. Blend the mix in a high-speed blender, then with the motor still going, slowly add the white wine vinegar, 1 tablespoon of olive oil, and 1 tablespoon of ice water. Keep adding water a tablespoon at a time until you reach your desired consistency.

Conchigliette with Porcini Mushroom Ragù

There is something that comforts me about standing over a pot for the best part of an afternoon, chopping, stirring, tasting, and tweaking, all in the name of ragù. I fell for this labor of love after reading Samin Nosrat's *Salt Fat Acid Heat*, and watching the accompanying Netflix show. I was in my early twenties, broke and directionless, but occasionally I would save up enough money to buy all the ingredients, and on a quiet Sunday I would methodically make enough ragù to feed an army. This version uses porcini mushrooms, which give it a deeply earthy and rich flavor. Note: This is not a 30-minute meal or a recipe to make when you are in a hurry—take your time with it. The shape of conchigliette is perfect for holding this sauce, the little shells filling up with rich ragù. But you are your own boss, and you may use whichever pasta shape you please.

Serves 6–8

½ cup olive oil, plus extra as needed

1 onion, finely diced

1 stalk of celery, finely diced

1 carrot, finely diced

1 leek, finely diced

5 garlic cloves, finely diced

sea salt and black pepper

4¼ oz dried porcini mushrooms

1½ lb fresh mushrooms (cremini, portobello, shitake, or oyster), grated on a box grater

¼ cup tomato paste

⅔ cup white wine

⅔ cup red wine

1¾ lb fresh tomatoes, blitzed into a purée

1 tbsp miso

1 tsp Marmite (optional), plus extra as needed

1 vegetable bouillon cube

a sprig of rosemary, 2 bay leaves, and a sprig of thyme

1. Start by making the sofrito. Put ¼ cup of the olive oil, all the onion, celery, carrot, leek, and garlic into a large saucepan over medium heat.

2. Season with salt and pepper and sweat the vegetables down for at least 20 minutes, until they are starting to color and becoming jammy.

3. Meanwhile, rehydrate the dried mushrooms in enough boiling water to cover.

4. Put ¼ cup of the olive oil into a separate large frying pan, over medium-high heat. Fry the grated fresh mushrooms until crispy and browning. You will need to do this in batches, and it will take some time—you want the mushrooms to brown, not just sweat. If the pan becomes dry, add more oil to stop the mushrooms from sticking.

5. Drain the porcini mushrooms, reserving the liquid, and finely chop to match the texture of the fresh mushrooms.

6. Fry the porcini in batches until also browned and crisp.

7. Back to the sofrito: add the tomato paste and keep cooking until it turns a deep red color and starts to caramelize around the edges, being careful it doesn't catch.

8. Add all the browned mushrooms, stir to combine, and let it sizzle together for a good few minutes.

1 tbsp sugar
a chunk of Parmesan rind*
ground nutmeg (optional)
1 lb conchigliette
grated Parmesan, for topping*

*Omit Parmesan to keep this recipe
  vegan

9. Add all the wine, the blitzed tomatoes, miso, Marmite (if using), bouillon cube, herbs, sugar, Parmesan rind, and a cup of the reserved porcini liquid. Bring to a boil, then turn down to a simmer and cook for 2 hours, stirring every now and again to make sure the bottom doesn't catch.

10. After 2 hours the sauce should have reduced and thickened, the flavors will have developed and matured, and your kitchen will be smelling divine.

11. Taste the ragù and adjust the seasoning—if you are me, that means adding a lot of black pepper, maybe a pinch of nutmeg, and perhaps even a little more Marmite.

12. Once you are happy, cook the pasta until al dente and drain, reserving a cup of the pasta water.

13. Mix half the ragù with the pasta, adding some pasta water and mixing vigorously over low heat to emulsify the sauce with the pasta.

14. Serve generously, with more ragù on top and an avalanche of grated Parmesan.

15. Some people like to hook the Parmesan rind out of the ragù before serving, but Virginia has taught me that it's very lucky to get the rind in your bowl of pasta, and so I like to let it stay in the pot, for luck and for flavor.

Orecchiette Pasta e Ceci

I made this for our 2023 Fall Supper Club at the warehouse and it was such a hit. Lots of people asked for the recipe, but this is the first time I have shared it anywhere. Good-quality canned chickpeas make a big difference in a recipe like this, where they really are the star of the show. There is no need to make your own pasta, but if you would like a slow Sunday project, I have included the recipe for handmade orecchiette too, for which you don't need any special equipment or skill, just time and patience.

Serves 6

2 white onions, very finely diced
2 carrots, very finely diced
8 garlic cloves, very finely diced
3 tbsp olive oil, plus extra for drizzling
sea salt
¼ cup tomato paste
2 sprigs of rosemary (left whole)
1 tsp chile flakes, plus extra as needed
black pepper
2 (15 ounce) cans chickpeas, including all their liquid
1 cup white wine
1 vegetable bouillon cube
1 lb pasta (I love orecchiette or conchigliette)
grated Parmesan, for serving (omit to keep this recipe vegan)

For the orecchiette:
2½ cups fine semolina, plus extra for dusting
¾ cup + 1½ tbsp warm water

1. Make the sofrito by sautéing the onions, carrots, and garlic in the olive oil with a pinch of sea salt. Cook the sofrito for at least 30 minutes—you want the veg to have softened, cooked down, and begun to color and caramelize.
2. Add the tomato paste, rosemary sprigs, chile flakes, and ½ teaspoon of black pepper. Mix well to combine and keep cooking for 10 minutes.
3. Add the chickpeas with their liquid, the white wine, and crumble in the vegetable bouillon cube. Bring everything to a boil, then reduce to a simmer.
4. Taste for seasoning and add more salt, pepper, or chile flakes if you think it needs it.
5. When you are ready to eat, cook the pasta until al dente, then drain and add to the chickpea mix. Stir to combine.
6. Serve immediately, topped with a generous helping of grated Parmesan, more black pepper, and a drizzle of olive oil.

To make the orecchiette:
1. Tip the semolina out onto a clean surface, make a well in the middle, and pour in the water.
2. Starting with a fork, mix the water into the semolina, using your hands to knead it into a dough, then work the dough for 10 minutes until smooth and supple.
3. Divide the dough into four equal parts. Cover with a damp kitchen towel while you are shaping, so it doesn't dry out.
4. Take one piece of the dough and roll it into a long rope. Cut the rope into small square pillows of dough, roughly the size of a blueberry.

5. Using the blade of a butter knife, take a square of dough and drag the knife over the top, applying a fair amount of pressure. This will give you a "little ear" of dough—turn the ear inside out and press gently over the tip of a finger. Place the orecchiette on a tray lined with parchment paper and sprinkled with more semolina to stop them sticking. Repeat until all the dough is used up. Let dry in a single layer for at least 1 hour and up to 3 hours.

6. Once the dough is dried out, either cook immediately or freeze, dusted with more semolina so that it doesn't stick.

7. Cook the orecchiette in well-salted boiling water for 2–3 minutes, until they float to the top of the pan.

8. The pasta will keep well in the freezer up to a month. When you are ready to use, cook from frozen, adding a minute or two to the cooking time. You know it's cooked when it floats to the top of the pan.

Pierogi

If you have never tried these Eastern European dumplings, I urge you to spend a slow Sunday making your first batch. Rolling, cutting, and filling this dough is one of the most therapeutic and calming ways to spend an afternoon, even better if you do it with a friend, halving the work and making time for a good catch-up while you are at it. I was first introduced to pierogi by my old head chef, Beta, at a staff party. The vegan filling noted below is inspired by the recipe she made for us. Then, a little while later, my housemate Wojciech had friends staying with us from Poland. To say thank-you, they spent a day making over a hundred pierogi. More than a delicious meal, the act of making them is so full of care and love that to me, they represent friendship and family above anything else. Nothing says "I love you" more than a piping-hot bowl of pierogi, with a dollop of sour cream, chopped chives, and an excessive amount of black pepper. To keep this recipe vegan, use sauerkraut in the filling instead of twaróg, and plant-based milk and butter throughout.

Serves 6–8

For the dough:
1 cup milk of your choice
½ cup (1 stick) butter of your choice
3½ cups + 3 tbsp bread flour
2 tsp sea salt

For the filling:
5 white onions, finely diced
1 tbsp butter of your choice
2 tbsp olive oil
sea salt
4 medium potatoes of your choice
1 lb twaróg cheese (or cottage cheese)
1 tsp ground nutmeg, plus extra as needed
black pepper

To make the dough:
1. Heat the milk and butter in a pan gently until the butter is melted.
2. In a large bowl, whisk together the flour and salt.
3. Make a well in the middle of the flour and pour in the warm buttery milk mixture. Starting with a spoon, mix the wet into the dry until a shaggy dough forms.
4. Once the dough is cool enough to handle, tip it out onto a clean work surface and begin to knead. Keep kneading for 10 minutes until you have a smooth dough.
5. Leave covered to rest for at least 30 minutes, or up to 4 hours.

To make the filling:
1. In a large frying pan, over medium heat, cook the onions with the butter, olive oil, and a pinch of salt. Keep cooking, stirring occasionally, for at least 40 minutes, until they have reduced, caramelized, and turned a golden-brown color.
2. Reserve half the onion mixture for serving and the other half for the filling.

To serve:

butter, for frying

1¼ cups sour cream (or a plant-based
   alternative)

reserved fried onions

a small bunch of chives, finely chopped

sauerkraut

cracked black pepper and sea salt

3. Boil the potatoes in their skins until cooked through, around 30 minutes, depending on the size of the potatoes. Drain and let cool.

4. Once the potatoes are cool enough to handle, peel the skins off with your hands and mash until smooth. Add the fried onions, cheese, nutmeg, 2 teaspoons of salt, and 1 teaspoon of pepper and mix well. Taste for seasoning and add more salt, pepper, or nutmeg to taste.

To shape and fill:

1. Divide the dough into four pieces and work one by one, rolling out each piece to roughly ⅛ inch thick, then cutting out rounds of dough, using a glass or cookie cutter roughly 4 inches in diameter. Keep working until all the dough has been rolled and cut into rounds. You should have 60–70 rounds.

2. To fill and shape the dumplings, take a round of dough and add roughly 1 teaspoon of filling to the center. Working from left to right, fold the dough over the filling to make a half-moon shape and pinch the edges together to seal. The amount of filling needed will depend on how big your round of dough is, and getting it right will come with a bit of trial and error.

3. Continue filling and wrapping until you have used up all the dough and filling. If you have leftover filling, store this in a container in the fridge for up to 5 days—it can be fried and eaten on its own.

4. Put a large saucepan of salted water on to boil. Working in batches of 4–6 dumplings, cook the pierogi for 2–3 minutes in the boiling water. Keep going until all the pierogi have been boiled.

5. You can totally eat the pierogi like this, with all the toppings, but I like to go one step further and fry them in butter to get a crisp exterior that complements the fluffy interior. Melt a little butter in a large frying pan and fry the pierogi for 2–3 minutes on each side, until they are crisp and golden.

6. Serve topped with sour cream, more fried onions, chives, sauerkraut, and LOTS of cracked black pepper and salt.

The Best Pizza You'll Make at Home

Like all the best dough-based meals, this is a mission requiring a few days and a bit of time. I would suggest saving it for the weekend, when you can enjoy the journey, invite some friends around, and have a pizza party at your leisure. Big thanks to Byron and everyone at Gazzo Pizza in Berlin for letting me come in for a day and soak up your genius. The dough requires an overnight pre-ferment, called a poolish, which provides flavor and rise. So, if you would like to host a pizza party on a Saturday night—get ahead with the prep on Friday!

Serves 6

For the poolish:
2½ cups / 300g bread flour
½ tsp instant yeast
1¼ cups / 300g warm water

For the final dough:
4¼ cups / 600g bread flour
1 cup + ¾ tbsp / 250g warm water
½ tsp instant yeast
1 tbsp olive oil
4 tsp sea salt
the premade poolish (see above)

For the tomato sauce:
1 (14.5 oz) can chopped tomatoes
2 tbsp extra-virgin olive oil
1 tsp dried oregano
1 tsp sea salt
½ tsp black pepper
½ tsp chile flakes

To make the dough:

1. The night before you would like pizza, make the poolish by combining the flour and yeast with warm water in a bowl. Mix well and leave covered at room temperature.

2. The next day, around midday, in a stand mixer with the dough hook attached, mix all the final dough ingredients, including the poolish, until well combined and homogenous. Mix on slow at first until everything is incorporated, and then speed up to a medium-high speed.

3. Keep mixing the dough for 10 minutes until you have a smooth elastic dough—you can also knead this by hand for 10 minutes with a good amount of elbow grease!

4. Cover and leave the dough to rest in an oiled bowl for 3 hours—this is called bulk fermentation.

5. At 3pm, stretch and fold the dough, leaving it covered at room temperature between folds. Repeat every hour for 2 hours.

6. Divide the dough into 8 equal parts, each weighing roughly 180g, shape each one into a tight ball of dough and leave on an oiled tray, covered, in the fridge until you are ready to cook. The dough can stay in the fridge like this for up to 48 hours, or you can freeze it at this stage if you'd like to save some for another day.

To serve:
⅔ cup / 100g fine semolina
3 (8 oz / 250g) mozzarella balls,
    roughly torn
a good chunk of Parmesan, grated
a bunch of basil
more olive oil, salt, and pepper, to finish

Equipment:
stand mixer

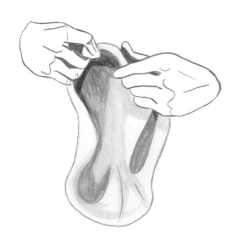

To make the pizzas and serve:
1. Take the chilled tray of dough balls out of the fridge.
2. Preheat the oven as hot as it will go and place a baking sheet on the top rack.
3. To make the sauce, blend all the ingredients together until smooth.
4. Take a ball of dough and toss it in the semolina, pressing from the middle outward, to flatten it into a disc, leaving the very edge of the round untouched—this will become the crust.
5. Stretch and shape the dough into a round with your hands—you are aiming to get as much air as possible out of the center of the dough and create a thin base with a crust around the outside. You can do this many ways— I like to let the dough rest on my knuckles, in boxer's hands, and turn the dough in a circular motion. This stretches the middle and keeps the crust intact, letting gravity do most of the work.
6. Lay the pizza base on a piece of parchment paper, and top with a spoon of sauce, spreading it evenly in a circular motion with the back of a spoon.
7. Add your preferred toppings evenly, making sure not to overload the pizza, as you can always add more once it's out of the oven. Finish with a light drizzle of olive oil.
8. Take the hot baking sheet out of the oven, transfer the parchment paper and the pizza onto the baking sheet and cook in the hot oven for 10–12 minutes. The cooking time will vary depending on the heat of your oven, how thin you have stretched the dough, and how many toppings you have added.
9. A bit like pancakes, the first pizza tends to be a tester, and once you have a sense of how hot the oven is and how long they take to cook, they will get better and better.
10. While the first pizza cooks, shape and prepare the second so it can go in as soon as the oven is free.
11. As soon as the first pizza is out of the oven, slice it up and dig in while the second one cooks. We tend to share each pizza as they come out of the oven, trying new toppings on each one, so that we all get to eat at the same time.
12. Repeat with the remaining dough and enjoy your pizza party!

Tomato, Spinach & Ricotta Lasagna

With the joint heaviness of béchamel and ragù, traditional lasagna is not for me. I like lasagna to be saucy enough that it doesn't feel dry, but secure enough to hold its shape when sliced and to possess visibly definable layers. I prefer this lighter, more summery flavor combination, that almost feels like a margherita pizza in a lasagna, and every time I make it for the warehouse it goes down a storm, not a leftover in sight. We served this at our Winter Supper Club in 2023 and it was the perfect cozy, warming meal for the dead of January.

Serves 8

For the tomato sauce:
7 tbsp olive oil, plus extra for drizzling
15 garlic cloves, thinly sliced
sea salt and black pepper
a large bunch of basil, stems finely chopped and leaves reserved
1 tbsp tomato paste
2 (14.5 oz) cans whole peeled tomatoes
2 cups passata (or tomato puree)
sugar (optional)

For the spinach and ricotta filling:
1 lb frozen spinach, thawed and squeezed dry
2 (15 oz) containers ricotta
2 eggs
1 (8 oz) mozzarella ball, grated
scant 1 cup grated Parmesan*
½ tsp ground nutmeg
½ tsp black pepper
1 tsp sea salt

To assemble:
10 oz dried lasagna sheets
2 (8 oz) mozzarella balls, roughly torn
2 oz grated Parmesan*

*Use another hard cheese to keep this recipe V

1. Preheat the oven to 400°F and grease a large ovenproof dish with a little olive oil.
2. To make the sauce, heat the olive oil in a large heavy-bottomed pan over medium heat. Add the garlic, with a pinch each of salt and pepper, and cook for 2–3 minutes, until they start to crisp up and get a little color.
3. Add the basil stems and tomato paste and continue to cook for another 3 minutes.
4. Add the canned tomatoes and passata, bring to a boil, then reduce the heat and simmer for at least 30 minutes.
5. Meanwhile, make the ricotta filling. In a large bowl, combine all the ingredients and mix until smooth and well incorporated.
6. Taste the tomato sauce and adjust the seasoning, if necessary, with a little more salt, pepper, or sugar.
7. To assemble, start by covering the base of the dish with a ladle of sauce. Next add a layer of pasta sheets, then another layer of sauce, and then one-third of the ricotta mixture.
8. Repeat this process until all the ricotta mixture is used up, then top the final layer of pasta with more sauce, the remaining mozzarella, Parmesan, and a drizzle of olive oil.
9. Bake in the oven for 30 minutes, or until the pasta is cooked through and the top is crispy and golden.

Ramps Tagliatelle, Butter & Parmesan

I first discovered and cooked with ramps (wild garlic) in the lockdown of spring 2020. I had returned to my family home in Ripon, north Yorkshire, and discovered a bumper crop by the river where we walked the dogs. My daily walks became foraging trips and I experimented with different ways of using this seasonal, fragrant green. There's nothing quite like a plate of fresh pasta; it's the most luxurious meal and if you have made it yourself you will have earned every mouthful. This is a labor-intensive meal, but one that I relish the chance to make. If you can't find ramps, or if it's simply out of season, this works very well with chives, which you can find all year round. I find this is a beautiful recipe to make around Easter, as the weather gets warmer and everyone's mood brightens.

Serves 6–8

3 oz ramps (or chives)
4¾ cups tipo "00" pasta flour
3 whole eggs + 3 egg yolks (to keep the pasta dough plant-based, substitute ¾ cup olive oil)
fine semolina, for tossing

To serve:
¾ cup (1½ sticks) butter, cubed
3½ oz grated Parmesan, plus extra as needed (use another hard cheese to keep this recipe V)
sea salt and black pepper

1. First blanch the ramps or chives in boiling water, refresh under cold water, then blend until smooth. Both ramps and chives are quite stringy, so don't worry if the purée doesn't come out completely smooth, it gives the finished pasta dough a beautiful pattern.
2. Tip the pasta flour into a pile on a clean work surface. Make a well in the center and add the ramp mixture, then crack in the eggs and egg yolks (or the olive oil, if using).
3. With a fork, start to whisk the wet ingredients into the flour, moving to a dough scraper and then your hands when the dough starts to come together.
4. Knead the dough for 10 minutes until silky smooth. This will feel like a long time kneading but it's completely necessary—persevere and you shall reap the rewards. Cover with plastic wrap and let rest for 1 hour.
5. Cut the dough into quarters and work with one quarter at a time, leaving the other parts covered so they don't dry out.
6. Using either a rolling pin or a pasta machine, roll the dough out as thin as possible, to the lowest setting on your machine or to ¹⁄₁₆ inch thick.
7. Then either with a sharp knife or an attachment on the machine, cut the dough into tagliatelle.
8. Once you have a fistful of tagliatelle, toss it in fine semolina and put to one side. Repeat with the rest of the dough.

9. Cook the tagliatelle in salted water for 1–2 minutes, in batches. Transfer to a large platter, sprinkle with the butter and Parmesan, and toss until all the butter and cheese is melted and incorporated.
10. Serve with more Parmesan, salt, and pepper.

In for Cakies

In for Cakies

My grandad David always referred to any and all desserts as "cakies"—he said it with the Yorkshire emphasis at the beginning of the word: "ca-kiz." He would wait just the appropriate and polite amount of time after the savory food to say, with a hopeful upper inflection, "Is there anything for cakies?" I never knew where this came from, but having chatted with my grandma Margaret recently, I learned that he had got it from her mother, my great-grandma Laura, who we knew as Little Grandma. Little Grandma was very fond of animals and was a farmer's wife living in the Yorkshire Dales. When the dogs were let out each day, they would run to her back door and she would say, "Come and have some cakies," which was, quite literally, leftover stale cake that was no longer fit for human consumption. Grandad found this rather amusing, and adopted the phrase himself, so I'm very pleased to be immortalizing it in this book.

When I was little I had an insatiable sweet tooth, but since moving to London and becoming a baker, my sweet tooth has abated—trying so much meringue every day hammered the sugar obsession out of me. Nowadays, I would always go for a starter and a main over a dessert. Having said that, my love for baking isn't going anywhere. We have two cake boxes in the warehouse kitchen and between Pier and me, they are almost always full, usually with banana bread, blondies, or cookies. I don't think I will ever move past my love for baking, I just can't help myself— if there are a few bananas turning brown in the fruit bowl, it's just a matter of time before they have been turned into a loaf. Nowadays, a dessert, cakie, or sweet treat has to be pretty spectacular, well-balanced, and irresistible for me to want to eat it over its savory counterparts. The following recipes are the exceptions to the rule and are on rotation in our warehouse.

Bars and cookies: quick and easy batch bakes that can be frozen, easily portioned, and shared
- Auntie Rach's Crunch
- Bakewell Pudding Slice
- Grandma Pat's Almond Macaroons
- Halva, Dark Chocolate & Sesame Cookies
- White Chocolate Burnt Caramel Cookies
- Masala Chai Shortbread
- Parkin
- PBJ Blondies
- Salted Popcorn Rice Crispy Tarmac
- The Best Millionaire's Shortbread There Ever Was
- Christmas Rocky Road

Cakes: from everyday loaves to showstoppers, there is a cake for every occasion
- Brown Sugar Vanilla Blackberry Sheet Cake
- Browned Butter, Almond, Summer Fruit Cake
- Burnt Basque Cheesecake
- Chocolate & Raspberry Sheet Cake
- Lemon Polenta Loaf
- Salted Chocolate Miso Torte
- Semolina Cake with Poached Rhubarb
- Slow-Roasted Bad Boy Cake

Desserts: from the everyday to the extraordinary, desserts to impress your grandma
- A Delicious Apple Crumble
- Bramble Fruit Sponge Pudding
- Citrus Sorbet
- Grandma Margaret's Raspberry Sponge
- Lemon & Passion Fruit Party Pavlova
- Sticky Toffee Ginger Pudding
- Tiramisù

Auntie Rach's Crunch

This recipe has very kindly been contributed by my auntie Rach. It has been tweaked, changed, and handed down through our family for years, my Grandma Pat making it first. You would be forgiven for thinking this is simply flapjack (a British oatmeal bar cookie) by another name, but you would be wrong. It's chewier, more buttery, darker in color, and altogether more enjoyable than a crumbly piece of flapjack. Crunch is good any time, but a piece midmorning, with a cup of tea, can improve the bleakest of days. It keeps very well in an airtight container and freezes well too, so I recommend always making the full batch, so you can have a stash on hand at all times.

A note from Auntie Rach:
"This recipe is requested at most family gatherings, but I never tire of making it and I always think of my lovely mum when I do. I took her recipe and completely changed it—but she approved and adopted my version!"

Makes 12 bars or 24 squares

1½ cups (3 sticks) / 340g unsalted
    butter of your choice
1½ cups / 340g dark brown sugar
6 tbsp / 120g Lyle's golden syrup (or
    molasses for a darker color and
    deeper flavor)
4¼ cups / 425g rolled oats
1⅓ cups + 1 tbsp / 170g self-rising flour
1 tsp sea salt

Optional additions:
2 tsp ground ginger
a handful of raisins, chopped nuts,
    mixed seeds, or all of the above!

1. Preheat the oven to 350°F. Grease a 9 × 13-inch baking pan and line with parchment paper.
2. Melt the butter, sugar, and golden syrup together in a small saucepan, stirring until fully melted and well combined.
3. In a separate large bowl, whisk together the oats, flour, and sea salt.
4. Combine the wet and dry ingredients, folding together until no dry spots of oats remain. Add the optional ingredients here, if using.
5. Pour the mixture into the lined pan and level out the top with the back of a spoon.
6. Bake for 20–25 minutes. It should be jiggly in the middle, crisp around the edges, and a golden-brown color—fear not, it will firm up as it cools!
7. Let cool for 10 minutes before cutting into bars in the pan, then let cool completely in the pan, before turning out and slicing fully.

Bakewell Pudding Slice

I went to school in Bakewell and one of my early weekend jobs was working on the counter at one of the three shops that all claimed to be the "original" Bakewell Tart Shop. There is much debate over the difference between the tart and the pudding, but the main differences are the pastry—pie dough for the tart and puff for the pudding. The filling is texturally distinct, the tart being a drier, cakier, more almond-y mix, and the pudding more of a custardy, jelly-ish, pudding-like (!) consistency. I like the pastry from the tart and the filling from the pudding, and my favorite way to eat it is in a neat square, from a larger bar cookie, like they sell in the shop. So this is my nostalgic, inauthentic, bastardized version of the famous Bakewell pudding—far better than the original, in my opinion.

Makes 12 slices or 24 squares

For the pastry:
1¾ cups + 2 tbsp / 245g all-purpose
   flour, plus extra for dusting
½ tsp sea salt
6½ tbsp / 80g sugar
½ cup + 1 tbsp / 130g unsalted butter,
   chilled and cubed
1 egg

For the filling:
2 whole eggs + 2 egg yolks
¾ cup / 165g sugar
½ cup + 3 tbsp / 165g unsalted butter,
   melted and cooled
1 tbsp almond flour
½ cup / 150g raspberry jam
a handful of sliced almonds

Equipment:
stand mixer (or electric hand mixer)

1. To make the pastry, put the flour, sea salt, sugar, and butter into the bowl of a stand mixer. With the paddle attachment, mix on a slow speed until the mixture resembles coarse bread crumbs. (Or simply mix and rub in the butter by hand.)
2. With the mixer still on low, add the egg and mix until it just comes together into a dough. If it seems too dry, add a tiny dash of ice water. Alternatively, mix by hand with a wooden spoon until it comes together into a dough.
3. Tip the dough out onto a floured work surface and knead briefly, then shape into a square. Wrap the dough with plastic wrap and chill in the fridge for 30 minutes.
4. Preheat the oven to 350°F. Grease a 9 × 13-inch sheet pan and line with parchment paper.
5. Roll out the dough to a rectangle shape, ¾–1¼ inches bigger than the pan. Line the pan so the pastry hangs over the edges—it might break or tear a bit while you transfer it to the pan, but don't worry, you can just patch it together with your hands. Trim the overhang, then put the pastry-lined pan into the freezer for 20 minutes to chill.
6. Line the frozen pastry shell with parchment paper and fill with baking beans, then blind bake for 20 minutes. Remove the baking beans and cook the pastry shell for 5 minutes longer.

7. Meanwhile, make the filling in a stand mixer or with an electric hand mixer, by whisking together the whole eggs, egg yolks, and sugar until thick, frothy, and doubled in size.

8. Gently whisk in the melted butter and almond flour.

9. Spread the jam evenly over the parbaked pastry shell, then pour the filling on top. Finally, sprinkle with the sliced almonds.

10. Bake in the oven for 15 minutes, then turn the temperature down to 325°F and bake for a further 30 minutes. Keep an eye on it so that the pudding doesn't brown too quickly on top, making a foil tent to cover if necessary. The filling should have firmed up but still have a jiggle to it.

11. Allow to cool completely in the pan, then turn out and cut into neat slices. Best served with a cup of tea.

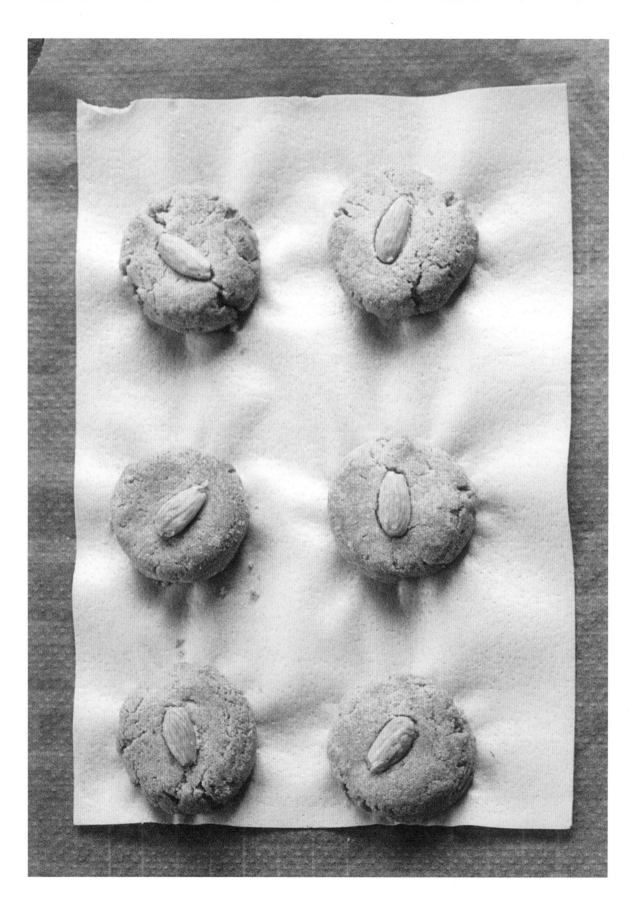

Grandma Pat's Almond Macaroons

My grandma Pat was a big fan of having a cup of tea and something sweet before bed, I guess just to round things out and send us off to bed with a tummy full of sugar—she called it supper. Often that sweet treat was an almond macaroon, and she would always have a stash of them in her freezer ready to go. These are far removed from the sickly-sweet, buttercream-filled French macaron, and are more similar to a coconut macaroon in texture. I have practiced and practiced, but, despite my best efforts, I can't seem to get them as good as Pat's. The rice paper is completely optional, it's what my grandma Pat and auntie Rach do, so for me it's nostalgic and has to be there, but they will be just as delicious without.

Makes 12 macaroons

3 cups / 340g almond flour
¾ cup + 2 tbsp / 170g sugar
3 egg whites
½ tsp almond extract
a few sheets of edible paper
    (rice paper; optional)
a handful of blanched whole almonds
    (if you can't find blanched, sliced
    almonds will do)

Equipment:
stand mixer

1. Preheat the oven to 325°F and line a baking sheet with parchment paper.
2. In a medium bowl, whisk together the almond flour and sugar.
3. In the bowl of a stand mixer, fitted with the whisk attachment, whisk the egg whites to stiff peaks.
4. Fold the dry ingredients into the egg whites, along with the almond extract.
5. Place a sheet of edible paper, if using, on the lined baking sheet and scoop out the mixture evenly into 12 macaroons. An ice cream scoop is a good tool for this, so you get them all an even size.
6. Flatten the scoop with the back of your hand to make more of a disc, roughly ¾ inch high. They don't spread too much in the oven, but allow ⅜ inch of space around each one.
7. Press half a blanched (or sliced) almond into the top of each macaroon, then bake for 30–35 minutes, rotating the baking sheet halfway through.
8. Remove from the oven and leave on the pan to cool.

Halva, Dark Chocolate & Sesame Cookies

Crunchy, chewy, salty, sweet, this cookie has it all. If you've never tried halva before, I highly recommend hunting it down—it's a sweet sesame treat that's sort of crumbly and soft in texture. When baked into this cookie it becomes a perfectly caramelized, nutty, chewy addition. You can find halva in most major supermarkets, but failing that, any Middle Eastern store will have it in abundance. These can also be cooked from frozen, and I always like to have a box in the freezer ready to go.

Makes 20 cookies

1 cup + 2 tbsp / 250g unsalted butter, softened
1⅓ cups / 300g light brown sugar
1 egg
7 oz halva, cubed
2 tsp vanilla bean paste
2 cups / 250g all-purpose flour
1 tsp baking soda
1 tsp sea salt
1½ cups / 150g rolled oats
    (1 cup / 100g blended into a "flour,"
    ½ cup / 50g left whole)
1 tbsp sesame seeds, plus extra for rolling
3½ oz / 100g good-quality dark chocolate, roughly chopped
flaky sea salt, for sprinkling

Equipment:
stand mixer

1. In a stand mixer, beat together the butter and brown sugar until just combined. Add the egg, 5 oz of the halva, and the vanilla and mix again until well combined, scraping down the sides of the bowl after each addition.
2. In a separate bowl, combine the flour, baking soda, salt, oats (both flour and whole), sesame seeds, and chopped chocolate.
3. Add the dry ingredients to the wet and mix until a dough forms, then shape the dough into 20 equal-sized balls, each weighing roughly 2 oz / 55g—I do this with an ice cream scoop so they are all the same size.
4. Roll each cookie ball in more sesame seeds. Using the remaining 2 oz of halva, press a piece of halva into the top of each cookie and put them on a lined baking sheet that fits in your freezer.
5. Freeze the shaped cookies for at least 1 hour, or until you are ready to bake. The cookies will last well in a container in the freezer for up to 3 months like this.
6. When you are ready to bake, preheat the oven to 350°F and line a baking sheet with parchment paper. Space the cookies out so they have enough room to double in size and sprinkle each one with a little flaky sea salt.
7. Bake for 12 minutes, then take the pan out and sharply tap it on a hard surface—this deflates the cookies and gives them a thin, crinkled texture. Put the baking sheet back in the oven for 3 minutes longer.
8. Let cool completely on the pan, or until they are cool and firm enough to handle—there is nothing quite like a warm cookie fresh from the oven.

White Chocolate Burnt Caramel Cookies

For me to enjoy white chocolate I need to contrast it with something bitter, and here that is the burnt caramel, topped with a pinch of flaky salt—these cookies are the perfect balance of sweet, salty, and bitter. They cook perfectly from frozen and so are a great bake to have in your freezer, pre-balled, ready to go—for that moment when you just need a cookie. Best of all, these cookies are very affordable to make, so it's a great recipe to look to when you need a bake on a budget.

Makes 12 cookies

For the caramel:
⅓ cup / 60g granulated sugar

For the cookies:
½ cup (1 stick) / 120g unsalted butter
1 cup + 2 tbsp / 150g all-purpose flour
1 tsp baking powder
½ tsp sea salt
½ cup / 120g dark brown sugar
⅓ cup / 60g granulated sugar
1 egg
1 tsp vanilla bean paste
5½ oz / 150g white chocolate, roughly chopped into chunks
a pinch of flaky sea salt

1. Line a baking sheet with parchment paper. Make the caramel by putting the sugar into a small saucepan over medium-high heat. Cook, swirling the pan until all the sugar has turned into a runny, dark brown caramel. If you have lumps of sugar not melting, use a wooden spoon or a heatproof spatula to stir and encourage everything to melt. Being very careful, as this caramel is roasting hot (!), pour it onto the lined baking sheet, set aside, and let harden and cool.

2. To make the cookie mix, melt the butter over medium-high heat, swirling the pan until the milk solids have separated and browned, around 5 minutes. Set the browned butter to one side to cool.

3. Meanwhile, whisk together the flour, baking powder, and salt in another bowl.

4. Beat together both sugars with the cooled butter until just combined. Add the egg and vanilla and beat until well combined.

5. Fold the flour mix into the wet ingredients, then fold in the chocolate chunks until just incorporated.

6. Roll the dough into 12 equal balls—they should weigh around 2 oz / 55g each—I do this with an ice cream scoop so they are all the same size.

7. Break the caramel into pieces and press a piece of caramel into the center of each ball.

8. Freeze the cookie balls for 30 minutes on the lined baking sheet—you can leave them in a container in the freezer for up to a month and just bake the number of cookies you want to eat at a time!

9. When you are ready to bake, preheat the oven to 375°F.
10. Place six cookies on a lined baking sheet, spaced out evenly to allow each cookie to double in size. Sprinkle a little flaky sea salt on top of each cookie. Bake for 11 minutes in the center of the oven, rotating halfway through.
11. Take the cookies out and tap the pan sharply on the counter a few times—this will make the cookies deflate and spread a little. Let cool completely on the pan. Repeat to bake the second batch.

Masala Chai Shortbread

This recipe is a marriage of two of my favorite things, masala chai and Grasmere shortbread. I was introduced to Grasmere shortbread by my family in Yorkshire. Apparently my grandma Pat made an excellent version, but it was a batch made by my auntie Rachel that I first tried and fell in love with. I had my first cup of masala chai while working in a boiling-hot underground kitchen in the heart of Delhi, where there was an urn full of the sweet, spiced tea that kept the kitchen crew caffeinated all day. Combining those flavors and textures here has produced one of my favorite cookies; paired with a cup of tea, there really is nothing better. My version is on the fiery side from all the spices, which I love, but if you prefer a more mellow flavor you can halve the ground ginger and black pepper quantities.

Makes 12 bars or 24 squares

1¾ cups / 240g all-purpose flour

1 tsp baking powder

1 tsp each of ground cinnamon, allspice, and ginger

½ tsp each of ground cloves, nutmeg, and black pepper

3 black cardamom pods, seeds removed and ground

a pinch of sea salt

½ cup (1 stick) / 120g chilled unsalted butter, cubed

½ cup + ½ tbsp / 120g brown sugar

2 tbsp molasses

2 tbsp Lyle's golden syrup

4 oz / 120g crystallized ginger, finely chopped or blitzed in a blender

1 tbsp granulated sugar

Equipment:
stand mixer

1. Preheat the oven to 325°F. Grease a 9 × 13-inch sheet pan and line with parchment paper.
2. In the bowl of a stand mixer, whisk together the flour, baking powder, all the ground spices, and the salt.
3. Add the butter to the dry ingredients and with the mixer on a slow speed, with the paddle attachment, mix until it resembles coarse bread crumbs.
4. Add the brown sugar, molasses, golden syrup, and crystallized ginger and mix on a medium-slow speed until it resembles wet sand, 2–3 minutes.
5. Tip the mixture into the sheet pan and level out into one even layer. Compress the mixture into one flat slab—to do this you can use the bottom of a glass, or a dough scraper. Or, if you happen to have another pan of the same size, this is perfect. Press down as hard as you can to really cement the mix together.
6. Sprinkle with the granulated sugar and press again.
7. Bake in the oven for 20 minutes.
8. Let cool in the pan for 15 minutes, then, while still in the pan, cut into bars or squares.

Parkin

Parkin is a traditional Yorkshire gingerbread cake often eaten on Bonfire Night, and for me, it is nostalgia in a bite. I have many fond memories of scraping the bowl clean and licking the scraps of batter off the back of a spoon after baking with my mum. If you have steel-cut oats, just pulse them in your food processor a few times to get them to a finer consistency. At a real push, you can use extra-thick rolled oats, again pulsed in a food processor, but if you can find it, a medium-grind oatmeal really is best. Parkin is meant to be made up to four days in advance and left to mature before being eaten—this requires great restraint and a level of forward planning not many are prone to, but I find even one night of resting improves the flavor and texture, so try to bake it the day before you want to eat it, if possible.

Makes 16 pieces

1 cup + 2 tbsp / 250g unsalted butter
½ cup / 150g molasses
⅔ cup / 200g Lyle's golden syrup
½ cup / 100g dark brown sugar
1⅓ cups / 150g medium oatmeal
    (or quick oats)
2 cups / 250g all-purpose flour
1 tsp baking powder
1 tsp baking soda
1 tsp sea salt
1 tbsp ground ginger
1 tsp pumpkin pie spice
½ tsp ground nutmeg
7 tbsp / 100ml whole milk
2 eggs

1. Preheat the oven to 325°F. Grease a 9 × 13-inch baking pan and line with parchment paper.
2. Melt the butter, molasses, golden syrup, and dark brown sugar in a saucepan over medium heat until just bubbling, then take the pan off the heat.
3. Whisk together the remaining dry ingredients in a large bowl.
4. Add the warm syrup mix to the dry mixture, folding it in until there are no more pockets of flour.
5. Whisk together the milk and eggs in a measuring cup and add to the batter, mixing until just combined.
6. Pour the batter into the prepared pan and bake for 50 minutes to 1 hour, until a skewer inserted comes out clean.
7. Let cool completely in the pan, then wrap tightly first in parchment paper, then in foil, and leave overnight, minimum, or up to 4 days. Then cut into squares and serve with a cup of Yorkshire tea.
8. This cake keeps well for up to 10 days in an airtight container.

PBJ Blondies

Peanut butter and raspberry jam has to be one of my favorite salty-sweet combinations, and it's a classic for a reason. I have opted to use frozen whole raspberries here, instead of jam, as I found the blondies were sweet enough themselves and that the whole fruit added a welcome acidity. Fudgy blondie, crunchy chunks of chocolate, salty peanuts, and a sharp hit from the whole raspberries—a winning combination.

Makes 12 bars or 24 squares

1¼ cups (2½ sticks) / 280g unsalted
    butter
1 cup + 2 tbsp / 260g light brown sugar
⅔ cup / 130g granulated sugar
2 tsp vanilla bean paste
3 eggs
2 cups / 260g all-purpose flour
1¾ tsp flaky sea salt
¾ cup / 100g salted peanuts
6½ oz white chocolate, roughly
    chopped
½ cup + 1 tbsp / 150g creamy peanut
    butter
1 cup / 100g frozen whole raspberries

1. Preheat the oven to 350°F. Grease a 9 × 13-inch baking pan and line with parchment paper.
2. Brown the butter in a small saucepan by melting it over medium-high heat and swirling the pan until the milk solids have browned to an amber color. Set aside to cool slightly.
3. In a large bowl, whisk together both sugars, the vanilla bean paste, and the cooled butter, then whisk in the eggs.
4. In a separate bowl, whisk together the flour and salt, then fold into the sugar mixture until well combined. Then add the peanuts and chocolate and stir again until well combined.
5. Pour the batter into the pan and smooth with the back of a spoon or spatula. Dollop the peanut butter over the top of the batter and swirl in with a skewer. Scatter the raspberries over the top and press each one down into the batter, so they are half submerged.
6. Bake for 40–45 minutes, until the edges are crisp and there is a slight jiggle in the middle. The cooking time ultimately boils down to a matter of taste—if you like a more fudgy blondie, it will take less time, if you prefer it to be a little firmer and crisp, it will take longer. Experiment until you find the perfect time to suit your taste.
7. Allow to cool completely in the pan, then chill in the fridge, ideally overnight, but at least for a few hours, before slicing into bars or squares. If you just can't wait to tuck in, then you can of course skip the chilling step, but I think it adds to the texture and definitely gives you a neater slice.

Salted Popcorn Rice Crispy Tarmac

"Tarmac" is a sweet treat I was served at school dinners, a bendy chocolate rice crispy square—I think it earned its name from its dark color and texture, which vaguely resembled a newly surfaced road. Whatever it was, it was delicious and very popular. For my version, I have added salty popcorn and cornflakes for texture, tahini for a deep nutty flavor, and a layer of set chocolate on top. I tend to save this bake for a big gathering, as it's on the pricier side with ingredients. This is the perfect bake to take to a party, to pop in the mail, or to have as an emergency treat in the cupboard—it's easy to whip up and lasts for up to two weeks, if you can hold on to it for that long.

Makes 12 bars or 24 squares

1 cup + 2 tbsp / 250g unsalted butter
1 cup / 300g Lyle's golden syrup
1 cup + 2 tbsp / 270g tahini
6½ oz / 180g white chocolate, roughly chopped
1 tsp sea salt
5¾ cups / 150g puffed rice cereal
3½ cups / 100g cornflakes
6 cups / 70g salted popcorn
7 oz / 200g dark chocolate, roughly chopped
6½ oz / 180g milk chocolate, roughly chopped
a pinch of flaky sea salt

1. Grease a 9 × 13-inch baking pan and line with parchment paper.
2. In a large saucepan over medium heat, melt the butter, golden syrup, tahini, white chocolate, and sea salt together until well combined.
3. Mix in the puffed rice, cornflakes, and popcorn.
4. Pour the mix into the lined pan and press it into one even, smooth, compressed layer.
5. Chill in the fridge for 10 minutes, to set.
6. In a heatproof bowl over a pan of simmering water, melt the dark chocolate. Once fully melted, take off the heat and stir in the milk chocolate until fully melted and cohesive.
7. Pour the melted chocolate over the chilled base, sprinkle with flaky sea salt, and leave in the fridge overnight to set.
8. When you are ready to serve, slice into bars or squares using a hot sharp knife.

The Best Millionaire's Shortbread There Ever Was

It's a bold claim, but I think I'm qualified to stake it, so hear me out. I had a phase of being obsessed with millionaire's shortbread, and set out to try every single option available. After extensive research, I concluded that the perfect version does not exist, so I made it for myself. My version is a combination of the healthier gluten-free bars and the full-fat traditional classics. I have made the base using nuts, oats, and maple syrup, which makes it naturally gluten-free. The caramel is more traditional, condensed milk deliciousness, and the salty dark chocolate topping balances everything out.

Makes 12 bars or 24 squares

For the base:
1⅓ cups / 150g almond flour
1¼ cups / 150g gluten-free rolled oats, ground into a "flour" in a food processor
⅓ cup / 70g maple syrup
¼ cup / 55g coconut oil, melted
1 tsp sea salt

For the caramel:
1 (14 oz / 397g) can sweetened condensed milk
1¼ cups (2½ sticks) / 300 g unsalted butter, cubed and softened
½ cup / 100g sugar
¼ cup / 100g Lyle's golden syrup

For the topping:
7 oz / 200g dark chocolate, roughly chopped
flaky sea salt

1. Grease a 9 × 13-inch sheet pan and line with parchment paper.
2. To make the base, blitz together all the ingredients in a food processor until finely ground and press into the pan in an even, smooth layer, compressing the mixture with your hands or a small rolling pin or the bottom of a glass. Chill in the freezer to set while you make the caramel, at least 15 minutes.
3. To make the caramel, put all the ingredients into a heavy-bottomed, shallow pan. Set over medium heat and stir continuously with a heatproof spatula, paying attention to the bottom and sides of the pan.
4. Once everything has melted, bring the mixture to a rolling boil for 5 minutes, stirring all the time, until the caramel turns golden brown. If the heat is too high, or you don't stir, the bottom will catch and you will find flecks of burnt caramel, so keep to medium heat and continue stirring. If the butter separates out, transfer to a heatproof bowl and whisk until it comes together.
5. Pour the caramel on top of the chilled base. Place it back in the freezer to cool and set for at least 1 hour.
6. Melt three-quarters of the dark chocolate in a heatproof bowl over a pan of simmering water. Don't let the water touch the bottom of the bowl. Once completely melted, take it off the heat and stir in the remaining one-quarter of dark chocolate until fully melted and smooth.

7. Pour the melted chocolate over the caramel, sprinkle with a pinch of flaky sea salt, and refrigerate to set completely—overnight is best, but at least 1 hour.
8. When you are ready to slice, use a sharp knife dipped in boiling water and wipe dry after each slice; this will help with cleanly cutting through the chocolate.

Christmas Rocky Road

Rocky Road is a Kellett family Christmas classic that my mum always makes, dusted with powdered sugar and decorated with little model reindeer, inspired by Nigella, of course. In this recipe I have included my favorite nuts—some salted, some plain—and I've opted for less traditional dried fruit, which for me really takes it to the next level. I have never been a fan of glacé cherries, but give me a prune paired with dark chocolate any day and I'm yours. This bake is on the more expensive side to make, but it is really a once-a-year thing and goes a long way, so it's worth the investment in my opinion. Please adapt this to suit your favorite nuts, fruits, and cookies—we should all be eating what we want at Christmas!

Makes 12 bars or 24 squares

For the chocolate mix:

12 oz / 340g dark chocolate

6 oz / 170g milk chocolate

⅓ cup / 100g Lyle's golden syrup

1 cup + 2 tbsp / 250g unsalted butter

For the dry mix:

1¼ cups / 200g dried cranberries

⅓ cup / 50g prunes, roughly chopped

⅓ cup / 50g pitted dates, roughly chopped

5 oz / 150g oatmeal cookies, such as Hobnobs, broken into bite-size pieces

7 oz / 200g rich tea biscuits (or shortbread cookies), broken into bite-size pieces

¾ cup / 100g shelled pistachios, roughly chopped

6 tbsp / 50g roasted salted almonds, roughly chopped

¾ cup / 100g roasted salted peanuts, roughly chopped

powdered sugar, for dusting

1. Grease a 9 × 13-inch baking pan and line with parchment paper.
2. For the chocolate mix, melt all the ingredients together in a saucepan over medium heat.
3. In a large bowl combine all the dry mix ingredients.
4. Once the chocolate mix is melted, pour it over the dry mix and stir until everything is well combined and coated in the chocolate sauce.
5. Transfer the mix to the baking pan, compressing the mix so that everything gets squished together into one even layer.
6. Chill in the fridge for at least 1 hour.
7. When you are ready to serve, use a hot knife to slice it into bars or squares and dust liberally with powdered sugar.

Brown Sugar Vanilla Blackberry Sheet Cake

I love a brown sugar sponge, and this is my go-to recipe when I am making a vanilla-based cake; unlike the classic Victoria sponge, this has a deep caramel flavor and almost toffee-ish quality from the brown sugar. The sponge of this cake is naturally vegan—to keep the whole cake so, make sure to use a plant-based butter in the frosting.

Serves 8–10

3 cups / 380g all-purpose flour
2 tsp baking powder
1 tsp baking soda
½ tsp sea salt
1½ cups / 350ml oat milk
2 tsp apple cider vinegar
1 cup / 200g dark brown sugar
1 cup / 200g light brown sugar
1 cup / 250ml vegetable oil
2 tsp vanilla bean paste

To decorate:
¾ cup (1½ sticks) / 250g unsalted
    butter of your choice, softened
5 cups / 500g powdered sugar, sifted
2 tsp vanilla bean paste
a basket (1 cup) of fresh blackberries

Equipment:
stand mixer

1. Preheat the oven to 325°F. Grease the bottom of a 9 × 13-inch baking pan and line with parchment paper.
2. Whisk together the flour, baking powder, baking soda, and salt in a large bowl.
3. In a separate bowl, whisk the oat milk, vinegar, both the brown sugars, the vegetable oil, and vanilla bean paste until smooth.
4. Make a well in the dry ingredients and add the wet, whisking the whole time in the same direction, to avoid any lumps.
5. Pour into the pan and bake for 1 hour, checking after 40 minutes, until a skewer inserted comes out clean. Loosely cover with foil if the cake is browning too quickly.
6. Let cool completely in the pan, running a knife around the edge after 10 minutes.
7. To make the frosting, beat the butter in a stand mixer fitted with the paddle attachment on full speed for 5 minutes until very pale and fluffy. Add half the powdered sugar and beat again until well combined. Scrape down the sides of the bowl, then add the rest of the sugar with the vanilla bean paste and beat on full speed until smooth.
8. Turn the cake out and spread the buttercream evenly over the top with an offset spatula, then scatter over the fresh blackberries.
9. I like to slice the sheet cake into finger slices and serve each slice on a flattened cupcake liner, making it a great bake for parties.

Browned Butter, Almond, Summer Fruit Cake

This cake is the epitome of summer: it's sticky, jammy, fresh, and not too sweet. The browned butter and ground almonds give it a beautiful nuttiness, and it's just dreamy with a dollop of crème fraîche on top, on a warm summer's day.

Serves 8 generously

1 cup + 2 tbsp / 250g unsalted butter
3½ cups / 370g powdered sugar, sifted
1¾ cups / 200g almond flour
⅔ cup / 80g all-purpose flour
a pinch of sea salt
7 / 220g egg whites (from 7 eggs; save the egg yolks for tiramisù!)
1 tbsp vanilla extract
1 cup / 100g berries
1 ripe peach, sliced into half-moons (canned also work well)
crème fraîche, for serving

1. Preheat the oven to 350°F. Grease a 9-inch springform pan and line the bottom with a round of parchment paper.
2. Melt the butter in a saucepan over medium-high heat and continue to cook until it starts to brown, swirling the pan and keeping an eye on it so it doesn't turn from brown to burnt. Once the milk solids have gone a nutty brown, take the pan off the heat, transfer the butter to a bowl to stop it from browning further, and let cool.
3. Whisk together the powdered sugar, almond flour, all-purpose flour, and salt in a large bowl.
4. Add the egg whites and vanilla and stir until combined, then add the cooled brown butter and mix again.
5. Pour the batter into the pan and put into the fridge for 15 minutes until the batter has slightly firmed up.
6. Sprinkle the fruit on top, pressing the berries and slices of peach halfway into the batter.
7. Bake for 1 hour 15 minutes, or until a skewer inserted in the center comes out clean, covering loosely with foil after 50 minutes so it doesn't brown too much on top.
8. Let the cake cool completely in the pan, then release the sides and serve the cake with a light dusting of powdered sugar and a dollop of crème fraîche.

Burnt Basque Cheesecake

I made, on average, two of these cheesecakes every week for nearly eight years while working at Meringue Girls, and I loved every single one of them. It's an incredibly simple dessert that will add endless glamour to your table and impress all your friends. Its relatively simple ingredients all happen to be quite expensive in today's world, so in the warehouse we save this cheesecake for birthdays and big celebrations, making it feel even more special. I've yet to meet anyone who loves it quite as much as my housemates Tom and Bee, so this one goes out to them. The key to getting a smooth batter is all in the scraping down of the sides of the bowl with a spatula, so while it's annoying, it is worthwhile.

Serves 8

2 lb / 900g full-fat cream cheese
1⅓ cups / 300g sugar
1½ tsp sea salt
6 eggs
1 tsp vanilla bean paste
1 cup / 200g heavy cream
1 cup / 200g sour cream

Equipment:
stand mixer

1. Preheat the oven to 375°F. Double-line a 9-inch springform pan and line with parchment paper, letting the excess paper hang over the sides of the pan.
2. In a stand mixer fitted with the paddle attachment, beat the cream cheese for a few minutes until loosened and smooth.
3. Scrape down the bowl, add the sugar and salt, and beat again for a few minutes until well combined.
4. Scrape down the sides of the bowl again, then add the eggs, one at a time, mixing on a slow speed and scraping the bowl down between additions.
5. In a small bowl, combine the vanilla bean paste, heavy cream, and sour cream until smooth.
6. Finally, with the mixer on a low speed, pour in the cream mixture, allowing it to incorporate fully before turning the mixer off, scraping down the sides of the bowl and mixing a final time.
7. Pour the batter into the lined pan and sharply tap on a counter to get out any air bubbles.
8. Bake in the oven for 40 minutes. At this point the cake will still be very jiggly and just starting to color on the top.
9. Turn the oven up to 500°F for another 5–10 minutes, to caramelize the top. Keep a close eye on the cake at this point—the speed at which it browns will depend on how hot your oven gets and also how far you want to take it.

I like mine quite dark, and the more you make this cake, the braver you will feel about "burning" the top.

10. Let cool completely in the pan, ideally overnight—the cake continues to cook as it cools, and this really isn't one you can get away with serving a bit warm. Once at room temperature, chill in the fridge until ready to serve.

Chocolate & Raspberry Sheet Cake

This is hands down the most delicious chocolate cake I have ever eaten, and that's coming from someone who doesn't really like cake. It's oil-based, naturally vegan, and incredibly moist. Here I've topped it with coconut cream ganache and fresh raspberries, which cut through all the chocolate. I encourage you to play around with the toppings: I have done versions with peanut butter, salted caramel, and praline; the options are endless.

Serves 6–8

2 cups / 250g all-purpose flour
1⅓ cups / 125g cocoa powder
1 tbsp baking powder
1 tsp baking soda
½ tsp sea salt
1½ cups / 350ml oat milk
2 tsp apple cider vinegar
1 cup / 200g dark brown sugar
1 cup / 200g light brown sugar
1 cup / 250ml melted coconut oil
2 tsp vanilla bean paste
1 cup / 200g plain vegan yogurt

For the ganache:
1½ cups / 320g canned coconut cream (not milk!)
11 oz / 320g good-quality vegan dark chocolate, roughly chopped

For serving:
7 oz (about 2 cups) / 200g fresh raspberries

1. Preheat the oven to 325°F. Grease a 9 × 13-inch baking pan and line the bottom with parchment paper.
2. Whisk together the flour, cocoa powder, baking powder, baking soda, and salt in a large bowl.
3. In a separate bowl whisk the oat milk, apple cider vinegar, both brown sugars, melted coconut oil, and vanilla bean paste until smooth.
4. Make a well in the dry ingredients and add the wet, whisking the whole time in the same direction, to avoid any lumps.
5. Finally add the yogurt and mix until smooth.
6. Pour the batter into the lined pan and bake for 1 hour, checking after 40 minutes, until a skewer inserted comes out clean. This batter is super runny, so can sometimes take longer—if you see it browning too much, lay a sheet of foil over the cake to stop the top burning before the middle is cooked.
7. Let cool in the pan completely, then turn out onto a board or platter.
8. To make the ganache, place the chocolate in a heatproof bowl. Heat the coconut cream until just under a boil, then pour over the chocolate, and mix until it has fully melted and you have one cohesive ganache.
9. Allow the ganache to cool until it has thickened to a spreadable consistency, then top the cake generously and sprinkle with the fresh raspberries.
10. I like to slice the sheet cake into finger slices and serve each slice on a flattened cupcake liner.

Lemon Polenta Loaf

This cake is my idea of a perfect lemon drizzle loaf—it's drenched in a lemon syrup while still warm to give it that squidgy sticky vibe, and the polenta gives it a really pleasing, slightly crunchy texture. It's ideal with a cup of tea and also for breakfast, and just honestly for any time of the day. It's easy, speedy, and just so happens to be gluten-free.

Serves 6–8

For the cake:
¾ cup + 2 tbsp / 200g unsalted butter, softened, plus extra for greasing
1 cup / 200g granulated sugar
1⅔ cups / 200g almond flour
¾ cup / 100g fine polenta (cornmeal)
1½ tsp baking powder
1 tsp sea salt
3 eggs
zest of 3 lemons

For the syrup:
juice of 1 lemon
½ cup plus 1 tbsp / 60g powdered sugar

To serve:
powdered sugar, for dusting
crème fraîche (optional)

1. Preheat the oven to 350°F. Grease a 9 × 5-inch loaf pan and line with parchment paper.
2. In a large bowl, beat the butter and sugar until pale and fluffy, at least 3 minutes.
3. In a separate large bowl, whisk together all the remaining dry ingredients.
4. Mix the eggs into the butter-sugar mixture one at a time, alternating with a scoop of the dry ingredients, scraping down after each addition, until all the eggs and dry ingredients are added to the mix.
5. Fold in the lemon zest, then scoop the batter into the loaf pan and level out the top with an offset spatula.
6. Bake for 50 minutes, or until a skewer comes out clean and the sides of the cake are pulling away from the pan.
7. To make the syrup, combine the lemon juice and powdered sugar in a saucepan over medium heat. Bring the mixture to a boil, then take off the heat.
8. Once the cake is out of the oven, prick it all over with a skewer and pour on the syrup.
9. Let the cake cool completely in the pan, then turn out, dust with powdered sugar, and serve in thick slices with a dollop of crème fraîche if you're feeling fancy.

Note: Don't be disheartened if the middle of the loaf sinks a little, this can happen, as the sides cook quicker than the middle.

Salted Chocolate Miso Torte

This chocolate torte is such a gem; it will save the day on any occasion when you need a dessert to impress, that maybe needs to be gluten-free, decadent, and quick to realize. The method is highly satisfying and very simple—although you do benefit from having a good electric hand mixer or stand mixer available, it's possible to do it manually with a fair amount of elbow grease. The texture of this cake improves over time, so it's a great one to make in advance. It's the perfect balance of salty, bitter, and sweet and I have yet to meet a person who doesn't love it.

Serves 10–12

6 eggs, yolks and whites separated
1¼ cups / 250g sugar
7 oz / 200g dark chocolate, roughly
   chopped
5¼ oz / 150g milk chocolate, roughly
   chopped
1 cup + 2 tbsp / 250g unsalted butter
¼ cup / 60g white miso
3 tbsp cocoa powder, plus extra for
   dusting
a pinch of flaky sea salt

To serve:
crème fraîche, optional

Equipment:
stand mixer (or electric hand mixer)

1. Preheat the oven to 350°F. Grease a 9-inch springform pan and line the bottom with a round of parchment paper.
2. In the bowl of a stand mixer, or using an electric hand mixer, whisk the egg yolks and the sugar until thick, glossy, and doubled in volume.
3. Meanwhile, in a heatproof bowl over a pan of simmering water, melt both chocolates, the butter, and miso together, stirring occasionally until combined. Once fully melted, take the bowl off the heat and set to one side to cool slightly.
4. In a separate bowl, whisk the egg whites until they reach soft peaks. It's important not to overwhip the egg whites— you want them still dropping off the spoon, almost the thickness of lightly whipped cream. If they are at stiff peaks, it becomes harder to incorporate them into the final cake mix and you end up with a lumpy batter.
5. Gently fold the cooled chocolate-miso mix into the whisked egg yolks, until just combined. Then fold in the egg whites in three additions.
6. Finally sift the cocoa powder into the cake batter and fold in until fully incorporated.
7. Pour the batter into the cake pan, sprinkle with a pinch of flaky sea salt, and bake for 50 minutes, or until the top is set but the cake still has a jiggle in the center.
8. Let cool completely in the pan.
9. Run a knife around the sides to loosen the cake, and remove the sides. Serve with more cocoa powder dusted on top and a dollop of crème fraîche (if using).

Semolina Cake with Poached Rhubarb

This simple cake is wonderful on its own, with a cup of tea, but is even better served as a dessert with this poached rhubarb and crème fraîche. At other times of year, when rhubarb is out of season, you could pair with a roasted fruit, such as pears, apricots, or grapes.

Serves 6-8

For the cake:
1 cup + 2 tbsp / 250g unsalted butter
1¼ cups / 250g granulated sugar
2 cups + 3 tbsp / 250g almond flour
¾ cup / 125g semolina
2 tsp baking powder
3 eggs
2 tbsp lemon zest

For the rhubarb:
1 lb / 450g rhubarb (trimmed weight),
    cut into 2-inch lengths
½ cup + 2 tbsp / 125g granulated sugar
zest of 1 orange, peeled in strips
enough cold water to cover the rhubarb

For the syrup:
⅓ cup / 80ml fresh lemon juice
1 cup + 3 tbsp / 120g powdered sugar

To serve:
1¼ cups / 300ml crème fraîche (or
    sour cream)

Equipment:
stand mixer

1. Preheat the oven to 350°F. Grease a 9-inch springform pan and line the bottom with a round of parchment paper.
2. In a stand mixer fitted with the paddle attachment, beat the butter and granulated sugar together until pale and fluffy, at least 5 minutes.
3. In a separate bowl, whisk together the almond flour, semolina, and baking powder.
4. With the mixer on a low speed, alternate adding a scoop of the dry ingredients and an egg, scraping down the bowl between additions. Keep going until all the eggs and dry ingredients are added. Finally add the lemon zest and gently fold in.
5. Pour the batter into the pan and level out the top with an offset spatula.
6. Bake for 45 minutes, or until an inserted skewer comes out clean and the cake springs back to the touch.
7. Poach the rhubarb by adding everything to a saucepan and cooking over medium-high heat for around 8 minutes, enough to bring the cold water to a very gentle simmer. Take the pan off the heat and leave it covered until completely cooled.
8. Meanwhile, prepare the syrup by combining the lemon juice and powdered sugar in a saucepan. Place over medium heat, bring to a boil, then take off the heat and let cool.
9. When the cake comes out of the oven, let it cool in the pan for 10 minutes, then prick it all over with a skewer and drizzle the syrup over the top.
10. Serve thick slices of the cake with a dollop of crème fraîche and the poached rhubarb and its syrupy juices alongside.

Slow-Roasted Bad Boy Cake

If you've never had the pleasure of eating a slow-roasted bad boy, let me introduce you to the perfect campfire snack: a banana, stuffed with dark chocolate, wrapped in aluminum foil, and roasted in the hot coals of a dying fire. The chocolate melts and caramelizes with the banana, transforming it into an indulgent makeshift dessert. I've taken those flavors and stuffed them into a cake, with the welcome addition of caramel.

Serves 6–8

For the topping:
3 bananas, peeled and halved
   lengthwise
1 cup / 200g granulated sugar
3 tbsp water

For the cake:
1 cup / 200g dark brown sugar
3 bananas, mashed
¾ cup / 200ml vegetable oil
⅓ cup / 115g plain yogurt
2 tsp vanilla bean paste
2 eggs
1¾ cups + 1 tbsp / 240g all-purpose
   flour
1 tsp sea salt
1 tsp baking soda
1 tsp baking powder
1 tsp ground cinnamon
4½ oz / 130g dark chocolate, roughly
   chopped

1. Preheat the oven to 350°F. Grease a 9-inch springform pan and line the bottom with a round of parchment paper.
2. Lay the bananas for the topping cut side down in the cake pan.
3. In a medium saucepan over medium-high heat, combine the granulated sugar and water, swirling the pan to encourage the sugar to dissolve. Allow to boil until the water cooks away and the sugar turns into a light brown caramel. Be very careful—the pan and caramel will be roasting hot!
4. Immediately pour the caramel over the bananas in the pan, in as even a layer as possible.
5. To make the batter, whisk together the dark brown sugar, mashed bananas, vegetable oil, yogurt, vanilla bean paste, and eggs.
6. In another bowl, whisk together the flour, salt, baking soda, baking powder, and cinnamon.
7. Fold the dry ingredients into the wet, then finally fold in the chopped chocolate.
8. Pour the batter on top of the banana caramel layer and bake in the oven for 70 minutes, or until the cake springs back to the touch and a skewer inserted comes out clean.
9. Let the cake cool in the pan for 15 minutes, then run a knife around the edges and turn it upside down, banana side up, to cool completely out of the pan on a wire rack.

A Delicious Apple Crumble

We all need a reliable crumble recipe in our lives. After much discussion and canvassing of opinion, I've concluded that a classic apple is the most popular flavor of crumble. But you can totally substitute the fruit with another of your choice. I love plum, apple, and blackberry (an iconic matchup) and there are the more adventurous landscapes of rhubarb or gooseberry (YUM) . . . the list goes on. It will surprise exactly no one that I like to balance the topping with a healthy pinch of salt, to please my savory salty palate. I also add oats and semolina for added texture. I'll forever associate a bowl of crumble with my grandma Pat, home, warmth, and love. When you eat this crumble, I hope you feel some of that warmth and love from me.

Serves 6–8

For the apple mix:

3½ lb / 1.5kg apples, peeled and
    roughly chopped (I like to use a mix
    of Granny Smith and Braeburn)
7 tbsp butter, cubed*
2 tsp vanilla bean paste
3½ tbsp dark brown sugar
1 tsp ground cinnamon
a pinch of sea salt

For the crumble topping:

1½ cups / 200g all-purpose flour
1 cup + 2 tbsp / 250g unsalted butter*
⅓ cup / 50g semolina
½ cup / 50g oats
2 tbsp flaxseeds
1 tsp ground cinnamon
1 cup / 200g granulated sugar
3½ tbsp light brown sugar
1 tsp flaky sea salt

To serve:

vanilla ice cream*, for serving

* use plant-based butter and ice cream
  to keep this recipe vegan

1. Preheat the oven to 350°F.
2. In a 9 × 13-inch baking pan or baking dish, toss all the apple mix ingredients together and bake in the oven for 25 minutes while you make the topping, stirring halfway through.
3. In a large bowl, rub the flour and butter together until they resemble coarse bread crumbs.
4. Add all the other crumble ingredients to the bowl and toss until well combined.
5. When the apples are out of the oven, they should be saucy and beginning to caramelize but still have some bite to them. Scatter over the crumble topping evenly.
6. Bake in the oven for another 30 minutes, or until the top is a crisp golden brown and the filling is bubbling up at the edges.
7. Let cool for 10 minutes, then serve with vanilla ice cream.

Bramble Fruit Sponge Pudding

This simple dessert was a favorite on family holidays in North Wales, where each summer the hedgerows would be laden with juicy ripe blackberries, just begging to be picked and eaten. It's not lost on me that foraging your berries for dessert is not top of everyone's agenda, or available to all, but it is a lovely way to spend a summer's afternoon and this dish is far more delicious when using fruit that is in season. The recipe below is scaled to feed a crowd but can be easily halved for a smaller group.

Serves 8–10

1 cup + 2 tbsp / 250g unsalted butter, softened
1¼ cups / 250g light brown sugar
6 eggs
2 cups / 250g self-rising flour
½ tsp sea salt
6 cups / 600g bramble fruit, such as blackberries or raspberries
Scant ½ cup / 85g granulated sugar
2 tsp vanilla bean paste
powdered sugar, for dusting
ice cream, for serving

Equipment:
stand mixer or electric hand mixer

1. Preheat the oven to 350°F.
2. In a stand mixer fitted with the paddle attachment (or using an electric hand mixer), beat the butter until light and fluffy, at least 5 minutes—set a timer!
3. Scrape down the sides of the bowl and add the light brown sugar, then beat again for 2–3 minutes.
4. Beat in the eggs one at a time, scraping down between additions. If the mixture splits, add a tablespoon of the flour to bring it back together.
5. Fold in the flour and salt.
6. Tip the berries into a 9 × 3½-inch deep soufflé dish, sprinkle with the granulated sugar and dot with the vanilla bean paste, then give the whole lot a toss and a mix.
7. Pour the cake batter on top of the fruit mix and level out with the back of a spoon or a spatula.
8. Bake for 45–55 minutes, or until the cake bounces back to the touch and a skewer inserted comes out clean.
9. Let cool for 10–15 minutes, so it's not so piping hot.
10. Serve warm, dusted with powdered sugar, with a scoop of vanilla ice cream.

Citrus Sorbet

We served this sorbet at our very first supper club at the warehouse in the summer of 2023, using Amalfi lemons, and it was the star of the evening. Big thanks go to Katie, who gave me a brilliant recipe as a starting point. This is my version, slightly sweetened and adapted for a smaller at-home ice cream machine. It goes without saying, you could totally make this without one and do the fork-stirring method, but you would end up with a more icy granita-style serve. If your ice cream machine is one with a bowl that goes into the freezer, make sure to freeze it for at least 24 hours. We served ours in hollowed-out lemons, which is a time-consuming and laborious job, but worth it in my opinion, for the drama. If you choose to go down that road, include the juice from the scooped-out lemon flesh in your citrus juice.

Serves 6–8

1½ cups + 2 tbsp sugar
4½ oz whole citrus fruit
½ tsp xanthan gum
1¼ cups freshly squeezed citrus juice
    (I use this recipe for all citrus, so use
    what you have or what you prefer:
    lemon, blood orange, grapefruit, etc.)

Equipment:
ice cream machine

1. To make the sorbet mix, first make a sugar syrup by combining the sugar with 1 cup plus 2 tablespoons of water in a saucepan. Place over medium-high heat and bring to a boil, then turn off the heat. Set to one side to cool.
2. Quarter the whole citrus fruits and remove any visible seeds. Then blitz the citrus pieces in a blender, skin and all, until you have a smooth pulp.
3. Combine the xanthan gum with a tablespoon of the citrus juice, to make a smooth paste, then in a large bowl stir together the sugar syrup, citrus juice, citrus pulp, and the xanthan gum paste until well combined. At this point, I like to use an immersion blender to give the mix one last blitz and make sure there are no lumps remaining.
4. Chill this mixture in the fridge overnight. If you are using an ice cream machine with a bowl that freezes, put it into the freezer at this stage.
5. The next day, churn the mix in the machine until it is pale in color, visibly thickened, and is clinging to the paddle, around 30 minutes. Transfer to a container and freeze until firm.
6. Alternatively, if you don't have an ice cream machine, pour the mixture into a shallow wide dish that can fit into your freezer. Freeze for an hour, then every 30 minutes

remove, stir and mash the mixture with a fork, mashing
any large frozen chunks. Keep doing this every 30 minutes, until you have a smooth frozen mixture. It will
take roughly 4 hours of stirring, mashing, and refreezing.

7. When you are ready to serve, allow the sorbet to sit at
room temperature until it's scoopable.

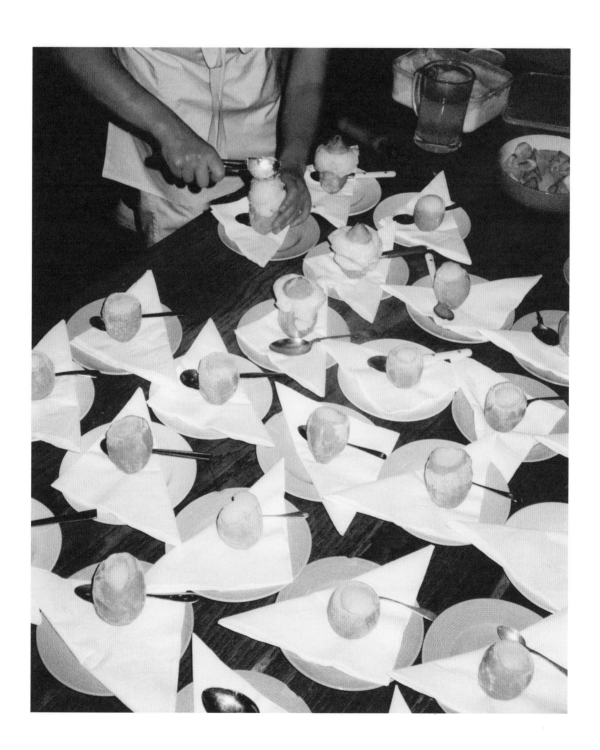

Grandma Margaret's Raspberry Sponge

This pudding is synonymous with my grandma Margaret and the week we would spend with her and my grandad David every summer. There wasn't a visit that went by that didn't feature raspberry sponge, and I have never had anything remotely similar since! I thought it was time to share this family treasure with a wider audience. As someone who doesn't love traditional cakes, this is what I ask for on my birthday and I look forward to it all year round.

Serves 12

1½ lb frozen raspberries
½ cup sugar
5 oz ladyfingers (the kind you use
   for tiramisù)
3¾ cups heavy cream
10 oz (about 2¾ cups) fresh raspberries

1. Set a large saucepan over medium-high heat and add the frozen raspberries along with 2 tablespoons of water. Allow to simmer until the fruit is completely thawed, broken down, and the liquid in the pan has doubled.
2. Take the pan off the heat and stir in the sugar until fully dissolved.
3. Set a sieve over a large bowl and pour the stewed raspberries into the sieve, without pushing the fruit through. Let them sit for a minute or two. Set aside the syrupy liquid that has gathered in the bowl.
4. Set the sieve over a clean bowl and push the fruit through the sieve to collect the raspberry purée, discarding the seeds left behind.
5. In a large bowl (preferably glass), lay the ladyfingers in a single layer to cover the bottom. Pour over all the reserved raspberry syrup—it may seem to be too much, but the ladyfingers will soak it all up in time.
6. Lightly whip the cream, until it just holds its shape. Take a scoop of the raspberry purée and gently fold it into the cream, then add the rest of the purée and fold it in until well incorporated.
7. Dollop the raspberry cream on top of the soaked ladyfingers and push it out in thick swoops, to cover the ladyfingers.
8. Decorate with the fresh raspberries, scattered atop the swoops of raspberry cream.
9. Chill in the fridge until you are ready to serve.

Lemon & Passion Fruit Party Pavlova

Along with introducing me to lifelong friends, my eight years as a Meringue Girl also taught me a few things about meringue. It's known as a notoriously difficult thing to get right, but really, if you take care over a few things, it is a breeze. Follow my tips and tricks below and you will be impressing your mates with towering pavlovas and perfectly crispy, chewy meringue at every party.

Serves 8

For the meringue:
6 / 190g egg whites, save the yolks for
   the curd
about 1¾ cups / 380g sugar (see step 2
   for more info)

For the lemon curd:
¾ cup / 180ml fresh lemon juice
   (3–4 lemons)
¾ cup + 1 tbsp / 180g sugar
180g eggs (start with the unused yolks
   from the meringue and top up with
   1 whole egg to make 180g)
1 cup + 2 tbsp / 250g unsalted butter,
   room temperature and cubed

To serve:
2⅔ cups / 600ml heavy cream
1⅓ cups / 200g unsalted shelled
   pistachios
6 passion fruits

Equipment:
stand mixer

Top tips and things to remember!
· Always use fresh egg whites, rather than cartons.
· When separating the eggs, take care that none of the yolk
   gets into the white.
· If the mix isn't thickening, add a teaspoon of cream of
   tartar once all the sugar is added and you are whisking
   on full speed.
· A stand mixer makes things SO much easier. It is possible
   with an electric hand mixer, but I personally wouldn't
   recommend it.
· Make sure all your equipment is completely clean, grease
   free, and dry.
· Make sure your oven really is at 200°F when baking the
   meringue—this keeps the color bright white and is the
   perfect temperature to get a crisp outside and a mallowy
   middle.
· If you are unsure about the accuracy of your oven, get an
   oven thermometer so you can be sure.

To make the meringue:
1. Preheat the oven to 350°F. Line two baking sheets and a
   6-inch round cake pan with parchment paper.
2. Weigh the egg whites, then weigh out exactly double their
   weight in sugar. This was tested with 190g of egg whites
   (from six eggs) and about 1¾ cups / 380g of sugar.
3. Put the sugar into the lined round cake pan. Put the egg
   whites into the bowl of the stand mixer with the whisk
   attachment and start whisking on a low speed. At the
   same time, put the pan of sugar into the oven.

4. Over the next 10 minutes, slowly crank the mixer up to full speed. By doing this slowly, you build a strong and stable mixture. You are aiming to have stiff peaked egg whites and hot sugar at the same time, after around 10 minutes. The time can vary depending on lots of things: the freshness of the eggs, the motor on your mixer, the heat of the oven, etc. The most important thing to watch out for is that the egg whites don't overwhip and separate into clumps. Check the sugar, and if it is hot to the touch but not yet caramelizing, then it's perfect. Take it out and turn the oven down to 200°F, leaving the door open for a while to help it cool down.

5. With the mixer still on full speed, slowly add the sugar, spoon by spoon, making sure there aren't any big hard lumps.

6. Wait for each spoonful of sugar to be incorporated before adding the next. Working slowly like this is another way you are building strength and stability in the mix.

7. Once all the sugar has been added, scrape down the bowl and keep mixing for another minute or two.

8. The mix is ready when it looks thick, glossy, and stiff. A good way to check is to turn the mixer off, dip a finger into the meringue, and see if you have a stiff peak when you pull it out; if the mix looks floppy, you need to keep going. The most daring way to check is to turn the bowl upside down over your head, and if you stay dry you know it's ready!

9. For a pavlova I like to bake the meringue in freeform dollops and then stack them into a tower, so spoon out the meringue into cloud-like shapes on the lined baking sheets—the less you interfere and touch the mix, the better.

10. Make sure your oven has cooled to 200°F, then bake the meringues for 3 hours. You can tell they are ready when they come away from the pan clean, with a crisp bottom.

(recipe continues)

To make the curd:

1. In a medium saucepan, whisk together the lemon juice, sugar, whole eggs, and egg yolks.
2. Set over medium-high heat and whisk constantly until the mixture reaches a boil and has thickened, about 5 minutes.
3. Take off the heat and whisk in the butter until fully melted and incorporated.
4. Strain the hot curd through a sieve and into a container.
5. Allow to cool completely before use, covering with a sheet of plastic wrap touching the curd to prevent it from developing a skin.

To assemble:

1. Whip the cream to soft peaks, roughly chop the pistachios, and scoop all the insides out of the passion fruits.
2. On a large platter, stack the meringue clouds into a tower, using the whipped cream as a sort of glue. Decorate with dollops of more whipped cream, lemon curd, passion fruit, and a sprinkling of chopped pistachio.

Sticky Toffee Ginger Pudding

This is my ideal version of sticky toffee pudding, heavy on the toffee sauce with a kick from the ginger. For the toffee sauce, you begin by making caramel, which is a little daunting, but I promise once you have mastered it you will be casually making caramel whenever your heart desires. This is ideal for dessert after a Sunday roast, on Bonfire Night, or truly on any cold winter afternoon when you need a little TLC à la STP (Sticky Toffee Pudding) to get you through the day.

Serves 10–12

For the pudding:

1 cup / 250g pitted prunes

2 pieces of stem ginger, finely grated, with 1 tbsp of their syrup

1¼ cups / 300ml strong black Earl Grey tea

1 cup / 210g dark brown sugar

¼ cup / 70g molasses

½ cup + 2 tbsp / 150g softened unsalted butter, plus extra for greasing

3 eggs

2 cups / 250g all-purpose flour

2 tsp ground ginger

1½ tsp baking powder

1½ tsp baking soda

½ tsp pumpkin pie spice

½ tsp fine sea salt

⅔ cup / 150ml whole milk

For the toffee sauce:

1⅓ cups / 300g granulated sugar

2⅔ cups / 570g heavy cream

¼ cup (½ stick) / 60g unsalted butter

1½ tsp flaky sea salt

vanilla ice cream, for serving

Equipment:
stand mixer

1. Preheat the oven to 325°F.
2. Soak the prunes with the stem ginger and its syrup in the strong black Earl Grey tea until softened, about 20 minutes. Set to one side.
3. Butter a 9 × 13-inch baking dish.
4. In a stand mixer, beat the dark brown sugar, molasses, and butter on medium speed until fluffy. Add the eggs one at a time, scraping down the bowl between additions.
5. Whisk together all the remaining dry ingredients in a large bowl, then with the mixer on a slow speed, combine the wet with the dry ingredients.
6. Take the soaked prunes and break them up with your hands so the mixture becomes more homogenous.
7. Pour all the tea, ginger, and prune mix into the batter and mix until well combined. Finally add the milk and mix until smooth.
8. Pour the batter into the baking dish—don't worry if it looks a little split or curdled.
9. Bake for 40 minutes. The pudding should have pulled away from the sides of the baking dish a little and an inserted skewer should come out clean.
10. While the pudding is baking, make the toffee sauce by putting half the sugar into a heavy-bottomed pan over medium-high heat.
11. At the same time put the cream into a small saucepan over medium heat.
12. Keep a close eye on both pans, gently stirring the cream so it doesn't catch—you don't want it to reach a boil, but just to get to steaming.

(recipe continues)

13. The sugar will gradually turn to caramel. If one spot is caramelizing quicker than the rest of the pan and threatening to burn, you can stir gently with a wooden spoon.

14. Once all the sugar is melted and amber in color, sprinkle the rest of the sugar on top of the caramel and repeat the process.

15. Once all the sugar is melted and no hard lumps of sugar remain, keep the pan on the heat, stirring and taking the caramel to a dark golden color. The darker you take it, the more bitter the resulting sauce will taste. I like mine quite dark.

16. Once you have reached your desired caramel color, very carefully pour the steaming cream slowly into the caramel, whisking all the time. There will be a lot of spluttering and steam, but persevere, keep whisking and gradually adding the cream until it is all in the pan.

17. Take the pan off the heat and keep whisking until the bubbles die down. Add the butter and sea salt and whisk until well combined.

18. Once the pudding is out of the oven, let it cool on a wire rack for 10 minutes, then prick all over with a skewer.

19. Pour half the toffee sauce evenly over the pudding.

20. Serve warm, with vanilla ice cream and the rest of the toffee sauce.

Tiramisù

I have never been a huge fan of this classic Italian dessert; I think perhaps I was put off by a few bad renditions, spiked with too much alcohol and coffee. Since living with my dear Italian friend, housemate, and collaborator Virginia Malavasi, I have been introduced to the sheer pleasure that a good tiramisù can bring. I highly recommend you give this version a go if you are a skeptic. I haven't included any alcohol, so everyone can enjoy it but also because I think that's often what lets a tiramisù down. If you insist on adding Marsala wine or another spirit, I encourage you to do so sparingly.

Serves 12

4 egg whites
8 egg yolks
2½ cups / 250g powdered sugar
28 oz / 800g mascarpone
1 lb / 500g ladyfingers
1⅔ cups / 400ml freshly brewed strong coffee, cooled
5 oz / 150g dark chocolate, finely grated
½ cup / 50g cocoa powder, for dusting

1. To make the filling, whisk the egg whites to stiff peaks.
2. In another bowl, whisk the egg yolks and powdered sugar until thick, pale, and fluffy.
3. Gently fold the mascarpone into the egg yolk mixture. I like to do this with a balloon whisk, moving from the center of the bowl to the edges, as the mascarpone can be quite thick, but persevere gently and it will become smooth in the end.
4. Then gently fold in the egg whites, until you have a smooth, homogenous mixture.
5. To assemble, dip half the ladyfingers into the coffee and arrange them in an even layer at the bottom of a shallow 9 × 13-inch baking dish. Next add half the mascarpone mix, topped with half the grated chocolate and half the cocoa powder. Repeat this process with the rest of the ladyfingers, dipped in coffee, then the rest of the mascarpone mix, grated chocolate, and cocoa powder.
6. Chill in the fridge for at least 3 hours, or ideally, overnight.
7. A few hours before you are ready to serve, take the tiramisù out of the fridge and let it come up to room temperature.

Recipe Contents

Section	Recipe	Gluten-Free	Pescatarian	Vegan	Vegetarian	Page
Breakfast	The Granola	/		/		30
	Spring Summer/Autumn Winter Oats	/		/		33
	Korean-Inspired Marinated Eggs	/			/	36
	Confit Cherry Tomatoes & Labneh on Toast	/			/	38
	Blueberry Cornmeal Muffins				/	41
	Caramelized Banana Loaf			/		42
	Cheddar, Jalapeño, Chive Corn Bread with Maple Harissa Butter				/	45
	Date, Walnut & Oat Soda Bread			/		46
	Comté, Green Onion & Sesame Scones				/	48
	Hot Harissa Shakshuka	/			/	51
	Savory Corn French Toast with Cherry Tomato Salsa	/			/	52
	Sourdough Pancakes with Roasted Seasonal Fruit				/	54
	Semi Sourdough Pikelets			/		57
	Savory Buckwheat Galette	/			/	58
	Egg, Cheese, Anchovy, Spinach Breakfast Muffin		/			62
	Brown Butter Mushroom Toast with Chives, Parmesan & Lemon Dressing	/			/	65
Lunch	Summer Holiday Bean Salad	/		/		70
	The Ultimate Chopped Egg Salad	/			/	73
	Tuna Salad	/	/			74
	Panzanella	/		/		77
	Beet, Black Lentil, Feta & Walnut Salad	/			/	78
	Crispy Chickpea Caesar Salad, Fennel Seed Croutons & Tahini Dressing	/			/	81
	Herby Vinegar-Laced Potato Salad	/		/		82
	Vermicelli Salad, Crispy Tofu & Satay Dressing	/		/		84
	Tofu Larb, Lettuce Cups, Abundant Herbs & Roasted Peanuts	/		/		87
	Spring/Summer Tomato Soup				/	88
	Autumn/Winter Tomato Soup	/		/		91
	Pearl Barley & Spring Vegetable Soup with Salsa Verde			/		92
	Roasted Carrot, Cumin & Coconut Soup with Cilantro Salsa	/		/		94
	Salt & Vinegar Potato Soup	/			/	97
	Bee's Potato Flatbreads			/		98
	Pier's Shrimp & Green Onion Pancakes		/			101
	Erbazzone Reggiano				/	104
	Potato, Mozzarella & Rosemary Galette				/	107
	Sourdough Focaccia, Three Ways			/		110
Dinner	Pantry Pasta	/			/	120
	Pantry Ramen				/	123
	Pasta Pomodoro	/		/		124
	Mushroom Pasta	/			/	126
	Pesto Pasta & Green Beans	/			/	129
	Spaghetti Puttanesca	/	/			130
	Sticky Eggplant Rice	/		/		133
	Okonomiyaki				/	134
	Brothy Fregola & Tomatoes			/		136
	Citrus Mackerel Spaghetti with Pangrattato		/			139
	Maple-Glazed Tofu & Garlic Fried Rice	/		/		140
	A Spring Pea Risotto	/		/		143
	Baked Beans				/	144
	Cheese Knödel				/	146

		GF	P	VG	V	
Dinner	Bee's Flammkuchen				/	149
	Sticky Sweet Potatoes, Tahini & Pickled Red Chile	/		/		153
	Roasted Asparagus, Lemon & Olive Oil	/		/		154
	The Hummus Plate	/		/		155
	Jammy Shallot Harissa Bulgur			/		156
	Harissa Honey Roasted Carrots, Tahini Yogurt & Sesame Seeds	/		/		157
	Hassleback Potatoes, Miso Almond Sauce, Massaged Kale & Lemon Dressing	/		/		158
	Sesame Spinach	/		/		160
	Last of the Summer Tomatoes, Roasted Squash & Brown Butter Hazelnuts	/		/		162
	Minted Garden Peas, Fava Beans & Sizzled Green Onions over Whipped Lemony Ricotta	/			/	164
	A Summer Feast			/		166
	Black Bean Chili & Charred Corn Salsa	/			/	170
	Cacio e Pepe					173
	Caponata, Fried Bread & Couscous			/		176
	Gnocchi alla Sorrentina				/	179
	Macaroni Cheese				/	180
	Potato & Pineapple Massaman Curry	/		/		183
	Roasted Squash, Browned Butter, Crispy Sage, Hazelnuts & Wilted Lacinato Kale	/			/	184
	Sri Lankan Dal with Coconut Sambal	/		/		186
	Mezze Feast			/		188
	Conchigliette with Porcini Mushroom Ragù			/		192
	Orecchiette Pasta e Ceci			/		196
	Pierogi			/		200
	The Best Pizza You'll Make at Home				/	204
	Tomato, Spinach & Ricotta Lasagna				/	208
	Ramps Tagliatelle, Butter & Parmesan				/	210
Cakies	Auntie Rach's Crunch			/		220
	Bakewell Pudding Slice				/	222
	Grandma Pat's Almond Macaroons		/			225
	Halva, Dark Chocolate & Sesame Cookies				/	226
	White Chocolate Burnt Caramel Cookies				/	228
	Masala Chai Shortbread				/	231
	Parkin				/	232
	PBJ Blondies				/	235
	Salted Popcorn Rice Crispy Tarmac				/	236
	The Best Millionaire's Shortbread There Ever Was				/	238
	Christmas Rocky Road				/	241
	Brown Sugar Vanilla Blackberry Sheet Cake			/		242
	Browned Butter, Almond, Summer Fruit Cake				/	244
	Burnt Basque Cheesecake	/			/	246
	Chocolate & Raspberry Sheet Cake			/		248
	Lemon Polenta Loaf	/			/	251
	Salted Chocolate Miso Torte	/			/	252
	Semolina Cake with Roasted Rhubarb				/	254
	Slow-Roasted Bad Boy Cake				/	257
	A Delicious Apple Crumble			/		259
	Bramble Fruit Sponge Pudding				/	260
	Citrus Sorbet	/		/		262
	Grandma Margaret's Raspberry Sponge				/	264
	Lemon & Passion Fruit Party Pavlova	/			/	266
	Sticky Toffee Ginger Pudding				/	271
	Tiramisù				/	274

Acknowledgments

To my mum and dad, Tim and Eleanor Kellett, thank you for raising me on delicious food, teaching me to appreciate where my food has come from, and for always being the most supportive, kind, and nurturing parents. A special thank-you to my mum, for providing almost every single prop; your crockery, linen, and cutlery collection is legendary, and I feel so lucky we got to borrow it for the pictures in this book.

To my siblings, Lily, Tom, and Grace, thanks for always being there, for making our childhood so special, and always fighting over the last sausage. To my little niece Agnes, thank you for baking with me, I can't wait to pass the baton on to you one day. To Josh, Jack, and Lau, thank you for loving my siblings and keeping them happy, for when they are happy, so am I. To my wider family, grandmas, grandads, aunties, uncles, cousins, and babies of cousins, you are the best and I feel so lucky to call you my family. May we always be obsessed with food.

To Rachel Mills, my wonderful agent, thank you for meeting with me on your vacation, believing in me, and sending me the best email I have ever received. You are the best kind of agent: kind, funny, achingly cool, and fiercely talented, I feel so lucky to be represented by you.

To Marianne Tatepo, Emily Martin, everyone at Square Peg, and the wider Vintage family; the *biggest* thank-you for taking me and my idea into the fold, it truly found its home with you. Thank you for nurturing this project into its final form, and for trusting me with so much of it.

To Raquel Pelzel, Darian Keels, and the wider team at Clarkson Potter, thank you for bringing *In for Dinner* to America; I'm still pinching myself and feel so lucky to be working with you.

To Andrea Villanueva de Milne, Harriet Connell, and everyone at the VTA, thank you for supporting, nurturing, and collaborating with me on, let's face it, everything! You are the best team and I feel so lucky I get to chat and work with you every day.

To Virginia and Benedikte, this book truly would not exist without you. I look back on that summer when we pulled together a proposal shoot in a day and I feel so proud; we worked with what we had, and we made something very special. You are both incredibly talented, hardworking, and kind, and I feel so lucky I got to work with you at the beginning of what will surely be stratospheric careers.

To David Pearson, thank you for bringing to life my vision for this book—working from a wine-stained tablecloth and a collection of Berlin architectural references, you have done wonders.

To my talented cousin Alice Kell, thank you so much for agreeing to illustrate this book. I have loved your drawings for a long time, and I am so thrilled to see them adorn these pages. Thank you for all your hard and beautiful work.

To Rhiannon Roy and Annie Lee for keeping such a tight ship with the copy edit and making sure nothing slipped through the net, you are wonder women.

To Stacey O'Gorman, you gave me my first job, taught me almost everything I know about food, and have inspired me in SO many ways over the years. Thank you for steering this ship and making my food look more beautiful than I ever could have imagined. You are correct on all levels.

To Sylvia Pearson, Isla Atkins, and Angus Vaughan, thank you for all your hard work on the shoot, keeping our teeny-tiny kitchen running smoothly and for all the washing up! You are the A-team.

To Claire Berliner, the London Library, and all the writers on the Emerging Writers Programme, especially Helena Pickup, Chris Fite-Wassilak, and Mark Henstock; thank you for giving me the time, space, feedback, and support to write this book. Claire, you allowed me to change lanes from a TV drama script to a cookbook; I'm sure that wasn't a pivot you had expected for this year's program, but I am so grateful that you ran with it, thank you.

To Clare Cole, thank you for testing with such precision, efficiency, and enthusiasm, I couldn't have done it without you!

To my long list of friends, family, and peers who signed up to receive and test these recipes as they were written, over the course of a year, thank you! You were the first people to read, make, and eat them, and your feedback was so crucial. Sending those emails out to you weekly and receiving your feedback made me feel so much less alone and like we were all doing it together, which I suppose we were. I owe you all a very large drink.

To the Supper Club crew: Virginia, Bee, Angus, Klara, Meg, Stacey, Frida, Lily, Pier, Wojciech, Manuela, Jake, Isla, Olivia, Manachain, Manuel, Ollie, Niamh, Lorella, Fergus, and Chris, thank you for being the best team. Feeding sixty-four people with you never feels like work, and I'm always sad to see you go the moment it is over. Thank you for being the best from day one. Merda, merda, merda!

To Sahara, thank you for being so good at your job and for helping me be better at mine.

To the warehouse family past and present: Bee, Frida, Tom, Virginia, Wojciech, Pier, and Chris, thank you for being the best housemates I could ever wish for, for being such diligent and committed taste testers, and for putting up with my 6am kitchen antics (sorry, Wojciech). You are, and will always be, my found family. This book wouldn't exist without you.

Index

Almond Macaroons.

6oz Gr. Almonds

3oz Sugar

2 or 3 whites of eggs.

Mix Gr. Almonds and sugar in a bowl & if
liked a few drops of almond essence.
Beat the egg whites to a stiff froth
and mix the almonds etc. with this.
Make into small rounds and on
wafer paper on a greased baking
sheet. Press half a blanched almond
on each & bake slowly for 30 mins.

150 20 mins (or 140)

CLARKSON POTTER/PUBLISHERS

An imprint of the Crown Publishing Group
A division of Penguin Random House LLC
1745 Broadway
New York, NY 10019

clarksonpotter.com
penguinrandomhouse.com

Copyright © 2025 by Rosie Kellett

Originally published in the United Kingdom by Square Peg, an imprint of Vintage, part of Penguin Random House UK, London.

Library of Congress Cataloging-in-Publication Data
Names: Kellett, Rosie, author. | Klüver, Benedikte, photographer. | Kell, Alice, illustrator. Title: In for dinner : 101 delicious and affordable recipes to share / Rosie Kellett ; [photography by Benedikte Klüver] ; [illustration by Alice Kell] Description: London ; [New York] : Square Peg, 2025. | Includes index. Identifiers: LCCN 2024057251 (print) | LCCN 2024057252 (ebook) | ISBN 9780593799710 (hardcover) | ISBN 9780593799727 (ebook) Subjects: LCSH: Dinners and dining. | Low budget cooking. | Vegetarian cooking. | LCGFT: Cookbooks. Classification: LCC TX737 .K385 2025 (print) | LCC TX737 (ebook) | DDC 641.5/52--dc23/eng/20250208
LC record available at https://lccn.loc.gov/2024057251
LC ebook record available at https://lccn.loc.gov/2024057252

ISBN 978-0-593-79971-0
Ebook ISBN 978-0-593-79972-7

Photographs: Benedikte Klüver
Illustrations: Alice Kell
Editor: Darian Keels
Designer: David Pearson | Production designers: Christina Self and Yasmeen Bandoo
Production editor: Sohayla Farman
Production manager: Kim Tyner
Compositors: Merri Ann Morrell and Zoe Tokushige
Food stylists: Stacey O'Gorman and Rosie Kellett | Food stylist assistants: Sylvia Pearson, Isla Atkins, and Angus Vaughan
Prop stylist: Virginia Malavasi
Americanization: Kate Slate
Proofreaders: Rachel Holzman, Erica Rose, and Eldes Tran
Publicist: Jina Stanfill | Marketer: Andrea Portanova

Author photograph: Kyle de Vre

Manufactured in China

10 9 8 7 6 5 4 3 2 1

First US Edition

The authorized representative in the EU for product safety and compliance is Penguin Random House Ireland, Morrison Chambers, 32 Nassau Street, Dublin D02 YH68, Ireland, https://eu-contact.penguin.ie.